FAITH IN FLUX

Catholicism and the Dynamics of Witnessing in Today's Nigeria

REV. FR. NEIBO BONIFACE ACHOR

foreword by:
REV. FR. ZACHARIA NYAMTISO SAMJUMI
Secretary General,
Catholic Secretariat of Nigeria

Insights into Faith in Flux...
REV. FR. PROF. CORNELIUS AFEBU OMONOKHUA
Executive Secretary, Nigerian Inter-Religious Council (NIREC)
Secretary General, West Africa Inter-Religious Council (WA-IRC)

FAITH IN FLUX

Catholicism and the Dynamics of Witnessing in Today's Nigeria

REV. FR. NEIBO BONIFACE ACHOR

foreword by:

REV. FR. ZACHARIA NYAMTISO SAMJUMI
Secretary General,
Catholic Secretariat of Nigeria

Insights into Faith in Flux...

REV. FR. PROF. CORNELIUS AFEBU OMONOKHUA
Executive Secretary, Nigerian Inter-Religious Council (NIREC)
Secretary General, West Africa Inter-Religious Council (WA-IRC)

Faith in Flux

ISBN: 978-978-60907-8-8

Published and printed by:

Pen-Impact Writing and Publishing Enterprise
16 Adedoyin Rhodes-Vivour Close, Asokoro,
Abuja, FCT, Nigeria
Website: www.pen-impact.com
Email: info@pen-impact.com
Tel: +234 701 990 4999

Table Of Contents

Reviews

This book is coming at the right time when the world is beginning to question the ability of certain men and women of God to stand up for the truth. Just like the way he often preaches the Word from the pulpit, Fr. Nebo uses straightforward diction and simple sentence structures to connect with his audience of all ages and backgrounds. The humble and unassuming man of God who preaches the Word with fire and power of the Holy Spirit has once again sent a very important message that we have a collective responsibility towards ensuring that faith overcomes all obstacles. I completely agree with him that we have a duty to ensure that faith remains a "force for good in our beloved nation." I enjoyed reading this work and I am sure that you will enjoy and be blessed by it.

Dr. Marcus Edino,
Royal Roads University, Victoria, Canada.

In this timely book, which exposes the resilience and adaptability of the faith in a rapidly changing society, Fr. Boniface calls on Catholics—clergy and laity alike—to be courageous witnesses of their faith, transforming society through the power of Christ's love. This book is a must-read for anyone seeking to understand the evolving role of the Catholic Church, in collaboration with Christians of other denominations, in shaping the Nigerian landscape.

Rev. Fr. Michael' Leke' BANJO
Deputy Secretary General/Director, Pastoral Affairs
Catholic Secretariat of Nigeria.

Fr. Boniface Neibo has written an interesting and timely book. He reflects on Nigeria's sociopolitical challenges and the contributions the Catholic faith must continue to make to the country's ongoing quest for development and progress. Well-researched and beautifully written, it is, more importantly, an invitation to Catholics to take the faith more seriously and become more truly, as Vatican II document *Lumen Gentium* (par. 48) puts it, the sacrament of Christ's salvation to the world.

Rev. Fr. William I. ORBIH,
Ph.D. Scholar, Theology and African Literature
Notre Dame University, Indiana, USA.

Faith in Flux: Catholicism and the Dynamics of Witnessing in Today's Nigeria offers an insightful witness to Nigeria's complexities Versus Catholicism's vibrancy and influence in education, healthcare, politics, integral human development, interfaith relationships, ecumenism, social justice, etc. Fr. Neibo examines the challenges of harmonising Catholic doctrine with indigenous beliefs, the role of Catholics in political engagement, and transformative digital ministries amidst the gimmicks of Pentecostalism. *Faith in Flux* is a call to action for both clergy and laity to ensure the Catholic faith thrives even more in today's Nigeria.

Rev. Fr. Oliver T. AGBILE, S.T.L
Ph.D. Scholar, Biblical Studies,
Emory University, Atlanta, Georgia, USA.

Preface

"Faith in Flux: Catholicism and the Dynamics of Witnessing in Today's Nigeria" offers a heartfelt reflection on how Catholicism thrives amidst Nigeria's rapidly changing environment. This book is a journey through my lived experiences and those of millions of Nigerian Catholics from diverse cultural and sociopolitical backgrounds, showcasing enduring faith.

Growing up in Nigeria, I was surrounded by a vibrant blend of traditions and practices. Sunday morning hymns intertwined with the rhythmic beats of local drums, creating a unique symphony of devotion. As I matured, I witnessed the challenges and triumphs of practising Catholicism in a multicultural society. These personal experiences shaped the inspiring narrative of this book.

"Faith in Flux" explores the dynamics of Catholic witness in Nigeria, a nation rich in diversity yet with a resilient spirit. It journeys through the historical roots of Christianity and Catholicism, highlighting the Church's pivotal role in societal development, from education, healthcare, and human formation to politics and social justice. It addresses how Nigerian Catholics balance tradition with modernity and faith with public life, especially in the digital age.

Woven into this book are countless stories from Nigerians—young and old, laypeople and clergy—each reflecting unique struggles, moments of grace, and leaps of faith. These narratives highlight the resilience and adaptability of Nigerian Catholics, who are steadfast in their devotion amidst a shifting socio-political context.

I invite you to read "**Faith in Flux**" with an open heart. Reflect on the historical context, but also immerse yourself in the personal stories that bring this context to life. This book is a call to action for every Nigerian Catholic to embrace our dynamic faith, stand firm in our values, and boldly witness the love of Christ in all we do. May **"Faith in Flux**" inspire, challenge, and renew your commitment to our shared journey of faith.

Foreword

One of the characteristics of the ocean's dynamism is its ability to ebb and flow. In this way, one can say that the oceans are constantly in flux. However, faith in flux does not mean that it is continually changing. Faith remains, but those things that challenge us are constantly in flux. Every era and place has its context in which faith is challenged. Living in faith today certainly has many contextual situations to be braved.

As the Church in Nigeria delves into the dynamics of witnessing to the faith, it encounters the delicate dance between tradition and evolution. However, like a seasoned traveller, the Catholic Church adapts to shifting landscapes and other societal phenomena while preserving its core identity. The deposit of faith remains unchanging for all times and all peoples, but the ways and means of effectively evangelizing every land and every generation require adaptations. Faith in Flux: Catholics and the Dynamics of Witnessing to Faith in Nigeria Today addresses this phenomenon in relation to the Nigerian context.

Delving into the history of the advent of the Catholic Church in Nigeria, the author presents how the Church grew from strength to strength amidst challenging encounters with native cultures and traditions, Pentecostalism, socio-political challenges, etc., at different stages in her history. Current challenges include taking the Gospel to the digital space and mobilising the Laity for more active participation in the nation's political life. The Church's challenge has been interacting with these realities of the Nigerian context while remaining faithful to her mission and identity.

In addressing these challenges, the author recommends a collaborative approach, especially concerning other Christian denominations, and the employment of modern means of communication, including a strong presence in the social media space where many Nigerian youths are to be found. The digital space has become a missionary territory.

Faith in Flux: Catholics and the Dynamics of Witnessing to Faith in Nigeria Today invites the Clergy, the Religious, and the Laity to renewed commitment and collaboration in service of the Gospel in modern Nigeria. It encourages the Church to prepare herself for both present and future challenges given the current quick pace of socio-political, economic, spiritual and technological evolution in the world, all affecting the Church and her mission.

I encourage everyone to get a copy of this book, which I consider a worthy contribution to making the Christian—nay Catholic—faith more relevant and effective in today's Nigeria. I commend the author, Rev. Fr. Boniface Achor Neibo, for this worthy effort and wish that the ideas therein will help the Church in her evangelizing efforts.

Rev. Fr. Zacharia Nyamtiso SAMJUMI
Secretary-General, Catholic Secretariat of Nigeria

Insights into Faith in Flux...

The Church, through her members, the lay faithful and clergy, is called to sanctify the temporal order. The Church gives meaning to secular life as the light of the world and the salt of the earth. This faith is dynamic and always changing according to the signs of the time. Fr. Boniface Neibo Achor researched very profoundly on the flux of this faith in this book: Faith in Flux, Catholicism and the Dynamics of Witnessing Today's Nigeria. This book captures almost all the aspects of the life of the Church, from history, dogma, liturgy, contextual theology, inculturation, ecumenism, inter-religious dialogue, social justice, technological engagements, etc. This book is a confirmation of the fact that the Church is a sign of God's presence in the world. In this divine presence, the Church has journeyed through the Catholic faith to a point where this faith is now meaningful to the African Church. This is what the introduction of this book, "Historical Overview of Christianity in Nigeria," has achieved.

The Church and State work in collaboration; hence, the Second Vatican Council imposed it as a rule for the Church to promote human dignity through the welfare of the citizens in any nation. While the hierarchy of the Church is the voice of the voiceless in a country where there exists poor governance and failure of government, the hierarchy in the Church, through practical examples in ecclesiastical leadership, encourages the lay faithful to be a sign and instrument of God's presence by getting involved in partisan politics. Given that the baptized Christian shares in the common priesthood of Jesus Christ, the lay faithful need to make the world a heaven by his or her prophetic and kingly mission.

This mission calls for sacrifice in witnessing in the face of religious pluralism, persecution, political instability, cultural syncretism, internal conflicts, the rise of Pentecostalism, and the commercialisation of the faith. The author then moved to another chapter, "The Sailing of Faith and Culture in Nigeria". The different churches are mentioned in this exposition. However, the Catholic faith is unique in the sense that, the Church calls on the lay faithful to be faithful to the teachings of the Church and be natural in the human society. Therefore, the lay faithful are encouraged to take part actively in partisan politics with the sole aim of restructuring a corrupt political system with the manifesto of Christ. His or her selflessness with the love of the common good should propel him to profess: "*The Spirit of the Lord is upon me, because He has anointed me to preach the Gospel to the poor; He has sent me to heal the brokenhearted, to preach deliverance to the captives, and recovering of sight to the blind, to set at liberty those who are bruised.*" **(Luke 4:18)**.

This mandate given to Christians is so serious to the point that the Fathers of the Second Vatican Councils had to say: The Christian who shirks his temporal duties shirks his duties towards his neighbour, neglects God Himself and endangers his eternal life.[1] Fr. Neibo took this as a theme in the next chapter, "The Christian Faith and Political Participation in Nigeria". The great Philosopher, Plato, told the people that, "One of the penalties for refusing to participate in politics is that you end up being

1 *Gaudiuin et spes*, 7

governed by your inferiors"[2]. Socrates told the youths of Athens that, "The wise who refuse to rule should prepare to suffer the rule of idiots".[3] Eric Arthur Blair (George Orwell) told the people that, "A people who elect corrupt politicians, impostors, thieves and traitors are not victims...but accomplices".[4]

Because the clergy is not advised to take part in partisan politics and active business in the worldly sense. He has an obligation to support the laity in carrying out the mission of the Church in the civil society. The aim is to produce not just a Christian president but a good President whose aim is to be a saint like Saint Louis of France. This is captured in the next chapter, "The Catholic Priest and Advocacy for Social Justice". The Church is not enmeshed in the world but seeks to sanctify the civil society with the involvement of her members in good governance. Apart from politics, the Second Vatican Council calls on all Christians to be involved in the work of saving souls and making this world a better place. According to the council, "Let Christians follow the example of Christ who worked as a craftsman; let them be proud of the opportunity to carry out their earthly activity in such a way as to integrate human, domestic, professional, scientific and technical enterprises with religious values, under whose supreme direction all things are ordered to the glory of God".[5]

Talking about, the digital age and the call to authentic witnessing, apart from the mission of promoting education and running schools, the Church is up to date in modern technology. In a radio message of Pope Pius XII, on Christmas Eve in 1942, the Pontiff said that, "The natural law also gives man the right to share in the benefits of culture, and therefore, the right to a basic

2 *https://www.brainyquote.com*
3 *https://plush.ng*
4 *https://www.bing.com*
5 *Gaudiuin et spes*, 43

education and to technical and professional training in keeping with the stage of educational development in the country which he belongs. Every effort should be made to ensure that persons are enabled, on the basis *of* merit, to go on to higher studies, so that, as far as possible, they **may** occupy posts and take on responsibilities in human society in accordance with their natural gifts and the skill they have acquired.[6]

On the "The Dynamics of Faith in Contemporary Nigeria, the Church seek to encourage Christians to be good ambassadors of Jesus Christ when they have the opportunity to participate in civil governance and other professional duties that could enhance human dignity. In the meetings of the Nigeria Inter-Religious Council (NIREC), the Co-Chairman, Alhaji Muhammad Sa'ad Abubakar, the Sultan of Sokoto and President General of the Nigeria Supreme Council for Islamic Affairs (NSCIA), said that the political leaders in Nigeria belong to either of the major religious in Nigeria. This would mean that if the Christian in a leadership position does not want to bring shame to Christianity and the Muslim in a leadership position does not want to bring shame to Islam by promoting the values and virtues of their various religions, then, we shall have a society that is free of corruption and all forms of crime.

It is expected that Muslim leaders should encourage Muslims to participate actively in partisan politics to promote peace, which is the core value of Islam. This is where the call for collaboration and solidarity, by the author makes laudable sense. The Catholic Bishops' Conference of Nigeria (CBCN) created the department of "Church and Society" in the Catholic Secretariat of Nigeria to coordinate the work of the Catholic Church in Nigeria as it relates to human society in general. This department promotes

6 Pope Pius XII, Radio Message, 1942

social development, human dignity, democracy, justice, equity, reconciliation and peace. In the context of dialogue of action, workers from different Christian denominations and other Faiths are employed to work in the Department of Church and Society. The Catholic Caritas Foundation of Nigeria (CCFN) is in touch with other National and International Agencies irrespective of religious affiliation.

On "The future of Catholic Faith in Nigeria", the second Vatican Council declares that the mission of the Church is the mission of Christ.[7] This mission is to inaugurate the kingdom of God on earth and prepare the people of God for eternal happiness in heaven. This would enable men and women to share in the divine nature. This mission is to be directed by the Roman Pontiff, the Vicar of Christ and successor of St. Peter at the universal level, while the bishop on the particular level as the local ordinary, directs this mission on the diocesan level. The parish Priest directs the parochial level in the parish. The Magisterium is the teaching office of the Church. This enables the Church to be faithful to the true teaching of Jesus Christ. The primary mission of the Church is the salvation of souls, while the secondary mission is to enhance the temporal order.

The missionary focus of the Church goes beyond her members to people of other religions. The Church sees good political governance as a mission to promote justice and peaceful co-existence in the society. With justice in the distribution of social amenities and temporal goods, the world would enjoy lasting security that is often threatened by the greed of some rulers. What the world yearns for today, especially in Nigeria, is a leader who loves God and humanity above selfish desires. The future of the Catholic faith in Nigeria depends on the work of the

---

7 Lumen Gentium 3

Holy Spirit as manifested and revealed in the action of the Christ faithful.

Nigeria is rich in everything except good leadership. This is why religious leaders must remain the voice of the voiceless. They must avoid the temptation of being prophets only to the politicians from whom they hope to get material reward. We do not need to wait until we all accept the same theological perspective before we can work together. We can begin by working on the humanity that is common to all religions. If we cooperate with one another irrespective of our different divides, we can grow a better nation that would provide an enabling environment for the Church. The future of the Church in Nigeria is bright if she becomes an evangelized evangelizer.

Rev. Fr. Prof. Cornelius Afebu Omonokhua
Executive Secretary, Nigeria Inter-religious Council (NIREC)
Secretary General, West Africa Inter-Religious Council (WA-IRC)

Acknowledgments

With immense gratitude and a heart full of joy, I acknowledge the many individuals and divine guidance that made "**Faith in Flux: Catholicism and the Dynamics of Witnessing in Today's Nigeria**" possible.

I thank God Almighty for being my anchor through every challenge and triumph. To my dear parents, Sir and Lady John and Justina Neibo, and my siblings Marcus, Patience, and Augustine, your unwavering love and support have been my bedrock.

I am deeply grateful to my Bishops, especially His Grace, Archbishop Ignatius Kaigama, Most Rev. Dr. Anselm Umoren, MSP, and His Eminence, John Cardinal Onaiyekan. Your leadership, guidance, and inspiring lives of faith have greatly influenced my journey.

Special thanks to Very Rev. Fr. Dr. Zachariah Samjumi and Very Rev. Fr. Prof. Cornelius Omonokhua for their insightful words and to my dear brother Priests for their companionship and dedication.

To you, Rev. Fr Kenneth Amadi, Rev. Fr William Orbih, Rev. Fr. Cyril Adama, Rev. Fr. Nzeka Valentine, Rev. Fr. Ajegena Akumbu, Rev. Fr. Agbile Oliver, Rev. Fr. Joseph Obada, Dr. Marcus Edino, Dr. Christopher Obioma, Miss Victory Osaigbovo, Mrs. Jennine Igwe, Mrs. Ngozi Nwanta, thank you for their meticulous editing and invaluable comments.

Lastly, to you, who is holding this book in your hands, thank you for embarking on this journey of faith and understanding. Your curiosity and engagement bring this book to life, and I hope you find inspiration and insight in its pages.

Dedication

To my beloved Mum, Mrs. Justina Neibo, and Sir John Neibo, my Dad, whose unwavering faith and boundless love have been my guiding light, and to the unsung and saintly Catechists who tirelessly teach the Catholic faith and values with unwavering commitment and dedication in every corner of the world, and Nigeria in particular, sometimes with little or no encouragement, your quiet heroism and steadfast devotion inspire us all. This book is for you.

CHAPTER I

Historical Overview of Christianity (Catholicism) In Nigeria

Nigeria, a nation with rich and diverse cultures and religious heritage, has been a significant hub for Christianity in Africa. The history of Christianity in Nigeria dates back to the 15th century, with the arrival of Portuguese missionaries. However, it was not until the 19th century that Christianity began to take root, particularly with the arrival of British missionaries (Ayegboyin & Ishola, 2011).

The first Catholic missionaries arrived in Nigeria in 1862, and by the mid-20th century, the Church had established a strong presence in the country (Ojo, 2013). As Pope John Paul II noted, "Nigeria is a country of great importance for the Church in Africa" (Pope John Paul II, 1982); the Catholic Church in Nigeria has a strong commitment to nation-building and national development and has been a significant player in the country's religious landscape, with a strong commitment to evangelization, education, social justice, peace, intra- and interfaith relationship and collaboration and integral development of people and the nation.

Today, the face of the Church is gradually changing as times change as well. The Nigerian situation is complex and challenging. Archbishop John Onaiyekan noted, "The Church in Nigeria is facing a critical moment in her history" (Onaiyekan, 2015). The country's political instability, corruption, and violence have impacted the Church's ability to effectively minister to her flock (Economist Intelligence Unit, 2022). In contemporary Nigeria, Christianity faces numerous challenges, such as:

1. Religious pluralism: Nigeria is a multi-religious society, with Islam, Christianity, and traditional religions coexisting (Hackett & Grim, 2011), and this comes with its peculiar challenges.

2. Persecution: Christians in Nigeria have faced persecution, particularly in the northern regions, where Boko Haram's insurgency has led to the displacement of thousands and the destruction of churches, Mosques and communities (Open Doors, 2022).

3. Political instability: Nigeria's political landscape has been marked by corruption, violence, and instability, which influenced how well the Church was able to care for her flock. (Economist Intelligence Unit, 2022).

4. Cultural syncretism: The blending of Christian and traditional religious practices has raised concerns about the authenticity of Christian witness (Ukah, 2012).

5. Internal conflicts: The Church in Nigeria has faced internal conflicts, including disagreements over leadership, doctrine, and practice (McCoy, 2018).

6. The rise of Pentecostalism and commercialisation of the faith: This has become a major ill to the Christian fate in modern times, and Nigeria is not spared. The jest and mockery of the Christian faith, which has been turned into an arena for entertainment, is appalling.

Amidst these troubles, the Catholic Church in Nigeria remains a strong force, with a great commitment to evangelization, education, and social justice (Catholic Bishops' Conference of Nigeria, 2017).

"The Church in Nigeria is called to be a beacon of hope and faith in a country facing many challenges." (Pope Francis) Nigeria, a country of diverse cultures and religions, offers a unique environment for the expression of faith, and as Africa's most populous country, Nigeria's socio-political environment has a significant impact on religious activity. The Catholic Church, in particular, has played an important role in shaping the country's religious dynamics. As stated in the *Lumen Gentium*, "The Church is a sacrament, a sign and an instrument of communion with God and the unity of all people" (Lumen Gentium, 1964).

The growth of Christianity in Nigeria is a tale of resilience, adaptation, and transformation. The Catholic Church played a significant role in the spread of Christianity in Nigeria with the arrival of Catholic missionaries in the 19th century (Ojo, 2013). The missionary, led by Priests like Father Joseph Lutz, established the first Catholic mission in Nigeria in 1862 (Lutz, 1889). As the Catholic Church grew in Nigeria, Catholic Priests played a crucial role in evangelization, education, and healthcare (Catholic Bishops' Conference of Nigeria, 2017). They established schools, hospitals, and churches and worked to promote social justice and human development (Ukah, 2012).

With the arrival of British missionaries and the establishment of the Church Missionary Society (CMS) in 1804, Christianity began to take root in Nigeria (Ayegboyin & Ishola, 2011). The CMS played a significant role in the spread of Christianity in

Nigeria, with missionaries such as Henry Townsend and Samuel Crowther working tirelessly to evangelize and educate the Nigerian people (Crowther, 1859). The establishment of the first Nigerian Church, the Holy Trinity Church, in 1842 marked a significant milestone in the growth of Christianity in Nigeria (Ojo, 2013). These early efforts faced serious challenges due to cultural differences, disease, and community resistance.

The 19th century marked a turning point in the spread of Christianity in Nigeria, especially with the increasing presence of European colonial powers. The British colonial government played a decisive role in promoting the activities of Christian missionaries. These missionaries, primarily from Europe and North America, began their mission to spread the Gospel and provide education and medical care to the local population. During this period, various missionary organisations emerged, including the Church Missionary Society (CMS), the Wesleyan Methodist Mission, and the Roman Catholic Mission.

Among the early missionaries, Bishop Samuel Ajayi Crowther stands out as a key figure in spreading Christianity throughout Nigeria. Crowther, the first African Anglican bishop, had a profound influence on Christendom. He was born in 1809 in Osogun (now Oyo State) and was captured and sold into slavery while still a boy. He was later released by the British Navy and taken to Freetown, Sierra Leone, where he was educated and converted to Christianity. Crowther's journey from slavery to bishop is a testament to the transformative power of faith.

Bishop Crowther's contribution to Christianity in Nigeria was significant and immense. One of his most notable achievements was translating the Bible into Yoruba, making it accessible to a wider audience in his local community. This translation work played an important role in spreading Christian teachings and integrating them with local culture. Crowther's efforts represented an early fusion of Christian doctrine with indigenous traditions and language, which helped to make Christianity more understandable and acceptable to local people (Isichei, 1995).

Missionaries' approach to evangelism often included establishing schools and medical facilities. Education was a powerful tool for conversion because it provided opportunities to teach Christian values. Mission schools became centres of learning and faith and produced many educated elites who later played important roles in Nigerian society. The emphasis on education also contributed to social and cultural change by challenging harmful traditional beliefs and practices.

Despite the positive impact of missionary work, there were also tensions and conflicts. The introduction of Christianity was often met with resistance from traditional religious leaders and practitioners. Many indigenous people feared abandoning their ancestral beliefs and customs. This resistance was sometimes strengthened by the colonial administration's support of missionary activities, which were seen as imposing foreign cultures and religions. The spread of Christianity in Nigeria also required negotiation of a complex social and political environment. Missionaries had to contend with local power structures, including kings and chiefs, who had enormous influence over the local communities. In some cases, alliances were formed with these leaders to promote the adoption of Christianity. However, these alliances were not always simple, as they involved finding a delicate balance between respecting local traditions and promoting Christian values.

Including biblical references in the story of the origins of Christianity in Nigeria helps emphasise the theological underpinnings of the missionary work. For instance, the Great

Commission in Matthew 28:19–20, where Jesus instructs His disciples to *"go and make disciples of all nations,"* resonates with the missionaries' mandate to spread the Gospel.

Additionally, the parable of the sower in Matthew 13:3–9 can be seen as a metaphor for the early missionary efforts in Nigeria, where the seeds of faith faced various obstacles but eventually found fertile ground.

Furthermore, official Church documents such as *Lumen Gentium* highlight the universal mission of the Church to spread the Gospel and serve humanity (Second Vatican Council, 1964). This aligns with the missionaries' dual focus on evangelization and social services. Similarly, *Nostra Aetate* emphasises the importance of dialogue and respect for different cultures and religions, reflecting the missionaries' efforts to engage with and understand the local context (Second Vatican Council, 1965).

The Development of Christianity

During the 19th and 20th centuries, Christian influence expanded significantly throughout Nigeria. Various denominations, including Roman Catholics, Anglicans, Methodists, and later Pentecostals, established a presence and built churches, schools, and hospitals. These institutions not only served religious purposes but also contributed to social development by providing education and health care (Falola, 2001). The emergence of these institutions marked a period of significant growth and change in Nigerian society.

In particular, the Roman Catholic Church played a crucial role in the development of Christianity in Nigeria. The Catholic Church's approach to evangelization was marked by her emphasis on education and social services, which resonated with many Nigerians. The establishment of seminaries and Catholic schools facilitated the training of indigenous clergy and the dissemination of Catholic teachings (Hastings, 1994). Catholic schools were known for their high educational standards and moral teachings, which attracted many families seeking a well-rounded education for their children.

One of the key figures in the growth of Catholicism in Nigeria was Archbishop Charles Heerey, who served as the Archbishop of Onitsha from 1934 to 1967. Heerey's efforts in expanding the Church's reach through the establishment of schools and healthcare facilities were instrumental in solidifying the Catholic Church's presence in Nigeria. His dedication to education and social welfare reflected the broader mission of the Catholic Church to serve both spiritual and temporal needs (Falola, 2001).

The influence of the Second Vatican Council (1962–1965) marked a significant turning point for the Catholic Church globally, including in Nigeria. Official Church documents such as *Lumen Gentium* and *Nostra Aetate* emphasised the Church's mission in the modern world and the importance of interreligious dialogue. These teachings influenced the Nigerian Catholic Church's approach to engaging with local cultures and other religious communities immensely and contributed to a greater level of impact and fruitful engagements. *Lumen Gentium* stressed the universal call to holiness and the role of the laity in the Church's mission, while *Nostra Aetate* highlighted the importance of dialogue and understanding among different religious traditions (Lumen Gentium, 1964; Nostra Aetate, 1965). The impact of these documents was enormous.

The Nigerian Catholic Church has begun to embrace more inclusive and culturally sensitive practices, recognising the value of local traditions and encouraging closer collaboration with other Christian denominations and sister religious groups. This period saw the growth of ecumenical or interfaith movements and interreligious initiatives aimed at promoting unity and mutual respect among Nigeria's diverse religious communities, and this has continued to this day.

The rise of Pentecostalism in the second half of the 20th century also had a significant impact on the Christian landscape in Nigeria. Pentecostal churches, with their emphasis on charismatic worship, emotionalism, miracles, and personal salvation, have attracted many believers. This movement introduced new dynamics into Nigerian Christianity, characterised by vibrant worship styles, flicks of emotions and a high-level focus on prosperity theology. The rapid growth of Pentecostalism challenged traditional denominations to adapt and respond to the changing religious environment.

Biblical references played a vital role in shaping the theological foundations of these developments. For instance, the Great Commission in Matthew 28:19–20, where Jesus commands His disciples to *"go and make disciples of all nations,"* served as a guiding principle for missionary activities and the expansion of the Church. Additionally, the emphasis on love and unity found in John 17:21, where Jesus prays for His followers to be one, underscored the importance of ecumenical efforts and interfaith dialogue. In the field of human service, the parable of the Good Samaritan (Luke 10:25–37) provided the biblical basis for the Church's commitment to health care and education. This parable, which emphasises the importance of compassion and caring for others, reflects the Church's mission to serve the underprivileged and improve the well-being of society.

The contribution of the Catholic Church to Nigerian society goes beyond spiritual nourishment. The establishment of hospitals, orphanages, and other social welfare institutions played an important role in meeting the population's needs for medical care and social welfare. A representative example is St. Petersburg in Onitsha. These include the establishment of the Charles Borromeo Hospital and the Catholic Hospital of Yiyi-Enu. These institutions provided essential medical services and served as training centres for healthcare professionals. Similar institutions and more have come up and are coming up till date in education, healthcare, humanitarian, etc.

Christianity and the Nigerian Society

The inculturation of Christianity in Nigeria has been a remarkable journey of faith and cultural exchange, shaped by the country's rich cultural heritage and the Catholic Church's commitment to evangelization (Catholic Bishops' Conference of Nigeria, 2017). As Pope John Paul II noted, "The Church in Nigeria must be truly Nigerian, yet truly Catholic" (Pope John Paul II, 1982). This call to inculturation has guided the Nigerian Church's efforts to contextualise the Gospel message within the local culture, promoting a vibrant and authentic faith experience (Ukah, 2012).

Inculturation has enabled the Nigerian Church to embrace the country's cultural diversity, incorporating traditional music, dance, and art into liturgical celebrations (Ojo, 2013). This cultural exchange has enriched the Church's worship and witness, making the Gospel more accessible and meaningful to the Nigerian people (Catholic Bishops' Conference of Nigeria, 2017). Archbishop John Onaiyekan observed, "Inculturation is not just a matter of adapting the Church's teachings to local customs, but of allowing the Gospel to transform and enrich our culture" (Onaiyekan, 2015).

The integration of Christianity into Nigerian society has not been without problems. Religion had to overcome the complex interplay of traditional beliefs and colonial influences. Nigerian

Christians found ways to incorporate elements of local culture into their worship and customs, resulting in a uniquely Nigerian expression of Christianity (Peel, 2000). This blending of traditions allowed Christianity to resonate more deeply with local people, creating a rich tapestry of faith that respected both new and old faiths.

One important development was the growth of independent African Churches. These churches emerged as a response to perceived inadequacies in the missionary-led denominations, particularly around issues of cultural relevance and autonomy. The Aladura movement, for instance, emphasised healing, prophecy, and the direct experience of the Holy Spirit, reflecting a blend of Christian and indigenous spiritual practices (Anderson, 2001). The Aladura movement's focus on charismatic worship and spiritual gifts attracted many Nigerians who sought a more vibrant and experiential form of Christianity.

The growth of these independent African churches highlighted the desire for an authentic Nigerian Christianity that could address the spiritual and social needs of the people. This desire for contextualised faith led to the incorporation of local languages, music, and rituals into Christian worship. This process of inculturation was important in making Christianity more accessible and understandable to the Nigerian population. Acts 2:4 states, "*And they were all filled with the Holy Spirit; they began to speak with other tongues, as the Spirit permitted them.*" This highlights the importance of communicating the faith in a way that resonates with diverse cultural traditions.

The Roman Catholic Church has also adapted her practices to better fit Nigerian culture. Vatican II documents, such as *Lumen Gentium and Nostra Aetate,* played an important role in this adaptation. *Lumen Gentium* encouraged greater participation of

Nigerian Catholics in the mission of the Church by emphasising the universal vocation to holiness and the role of the laity. *Nostra Aetate* emphasised the importance of interreligious dialogue to promote respect and understanding between different religious traditions (Lumen Gentium, 1964; Nostra Aetate, 1965). These teachings encouraged the Nigerian Catholic Church to study more deeply local customs and traditions while preserving core Catholic doctrine.

Moreover, the Catholic Church's approach to social issues resonated with many Nigerians. The Church's emphasis on education, health and social justice is consistent with the needs of Nigerian society. Catholic schools and hospitals have become centres of learning and care, contributing significantly to the country's social development. This epistle is reflected in James 2:14–17, which speaks of the need for faith to be accompanied by works. *"What good is it, my brothers and sisters, if someone says he has faith but has no works? Can this kind of faith save them? If it does not have works, faith itself is dead."*

The social teachings of the Church, as expressed in her numerous documents, also offered a framework for dealing with the current issues facing Nigeria. For example, Pope Leo's teachings advocated for the rights of the marginalised and promoted economic justice. Pentecostalism, which began to gain prominence in the late 20th century, introduced new dynamics into Nigerian Christianity. Pentecostal Churches, with their emphasis on prosperity theology, healing, and miracles, attracted large numbers of adherents. This movement's appeal lay in its promise of personal and material transformation, which resonated with many Nigerians facing socio-economic challenges. The rapid growth of Pentecostalism challenged traditional denominations to rethink their approaches and address the evolving spiritual and material needs of their congregations.

In summary, the integration of Christianity into Nigerian society has been a dynamic and evolving process. The emergence of independent African Churches, the inculturation of Christian practices, and the influence of Catholic teachings from around the world have all contributed to creating a vibrant and diverse Christian environment in Nigeria. The Church's commitment to social justice, education, integral human and societal development, and health has further strengthened her role in Nigerian society. As Christianity in Nigeria continues to grow and adapt, it remains deeply rooted in both its indigenous heritage and global connections, reflecting the complex and multifaceted nature of the Nigerian faith.

Modern Christianity in Nigeria

Modern Christianity in Nigeria is a thriving and diverse phenomenon shaped by the country's unique cultural and religious landscape (Hackett & Grim, 2011). With over 80 million Christians, Nigeria has one of the largest Christian populations in Africa (Pew Research Centre, 2020). Rightly so, Pope Francis noted, "The Church in Nigeria is a young and vibrant Church, with a strong faith and a deep commitment to evangelization" (Pope Francis, 2015). This vibrancy is evident in the numerous Christian denominations, movements, and initiatives that have emerged in Nigeria, each with its own unique expression of faith (Ukah, 2012).

Modern Christianity in Nigeria is also characterised by a growing emphasis on social justice, human development, and community engagement (Catholic Bishops' Conference of Nigeria, 2017). Nigerian Christians are actively involved in addressing social issues such as poverty, education, and healthcare, inspired by the Church's social teachings (Ukah, 2012). Archbishop Ignatius Kaigama, in the same vein, observed that "…the Church in

Nigeria is not just a spiritual institution but a social and cultural force that shapes the nation's values and morals…" (Kaigama, 2018).

Today, Christianity is one of the major religions in Nigeria, with millions of adherents spread across various denominations. The growth of Pentecostalism in the late 20th century brought about a dynamic shift in the religious landscape. Pentecostal Churches, known for their vibrant worship styles and emphasis on prosperity theology, have attracted large followings, particularly among the youth (Gifford, 2004).

The Nigerian Catholic Church continues to play a significant role in the country's religious and social life. Encyclicals like *Evangelii Nuntiandi* have reinforced the Church's commitment to evangelization and social justice, guiding the efforts of the Nigerian clergy in addressing contemporary issues such as poverty, corruption, and interfaith relations (Paul VI, 1975).

In conclusion, it is evidently important to acknowledge and accurately believe that the historical development of Christianity in Nigeria has been marked by flexibility, expansion, and resilience. Since its introduction by Portuguese missionaries, Christianity has undergone a transformation, characterised by a strong Pentecostal influence, and has become a fundamental part of the Nigerian social landscape. As we continue to explore the dynamics of faith in Nigeria, it is important to acknowledge the profound influence of Christianity in shaping the country's spiritual and social landscape. We look up to the Catholic Church because it has stood for the transmission and preservation of truth throughout the ages.

Cultural Diversity and Religious Practices

Nigeria is a nation of remarkable cultural diversity, with over 250 ethnic groups, each with its own unique traditions, languages, and religious practices. This cultural mosaic creates a rich depth of beliefs and rituals that significantly influence the social and religious horizons of the country (Falola, 2001). Among these diverse groups, Christianity, Islam, and indigenous African religions are the predominant faiths, each contributing to the country's complex religious identity.

Traditional African religions in Nigeria are characterised by a deep connection to nature, ancestors, and a pantheon of deities. These religions often emphasise rituals, festivals, and ceremonies that are integral to community life. For example, the Yoruba people participate in rituals, honouring deities such as Orunmila and Shango to seek guidance, protection, and blessings (Peel, 2000). The Igala people of Kogi state have a rich tradition and belief in names given to children and events or places: *Ojoma*, which means God knows; *Oma'Ojo*, which means Child of God, etc. There are also values and vices that are promoted and forbidden, respectively. These practices emphasise the importance of maintaining harmony with the spiritual world, which is believed to influence daily life and social well-being.

Introducing Christianity into this context required a dialogue between indigenous customs and Christian teachings. Catholicism, in particular, sought to integrate local customs into its religious framework. This process of inculturation allowed certain cultural elements to be retained in Christian practice, making the faith more accessible and meaningful to local people. An example of this is the application of traditional music and dance to Catholic liturgical celebrations, which helps bridge the gap between established and new faiths (Hastings, 1994). More to this is the translation of liturgical texts into local languages, which makes worship more integral to local culture. For instance, the Holy Mass can now be celebrated in local languages and is comprehensible to all.

Scriptural principles also provided the basis for this integration. For example, St. Paul the Apostle's approach to ministry emphasised *"Being all things to all people"* (1 Corinthians 9:22). This scriptural foundation supports the Catholic Church's efforts to respect and include cultural diversity in its mission of evangelization. The teachings of the Church reflected in *The Teachings of the Church* emphasise the universal character of the Church while at the same time acknowledging the unique contributions of different cultures to the Christian faith (The Teachings of the Church, 1964).

Moreover, the Second Vatican Council's document, *Nostra Aetate*, emphasises the importance of interreligious dialogue and respect for other religious traditions. It states, "The Catholic Church rejects nothing that is true and holy in these religions" (Nostra Aetate, 1965). This acknowledgement fosters a spirit of mutual respect and understanding between Catholics and adherents of other faiths, promoting peaceful coexistence and collaboration in Nigeria's pluralistic society.

The intersection of Catholicism with Nigerian cultural and religious practices is also evident in the Church's social teachings. The Church's commitment to social justice, education, and healthcare resonates with traditional African values of communal support and responsibility. For example, Catholic social services often collaborate with local communities to provide essential services, reflecting the biblical mandate to *"love your neighbour as yourself"* (Mark 12:31).

Furthermore, the rise of Pentecostalism in Nigeria has introduced new dynamics into this intersection. Pentecostal churches often emphasise spiritual experiences, prosperity, and healing, which appeal to many Nigerians. This movement's growth has influenced other Christian denominations, including Catholicism, to adopt more vibrant worship styles and address the spiritual and material needs of their congregations more effectively (Anderson, 2001).

Catholic responses to these trends have included a renewed emphasis on charismatic movements within the Church, promoting the gifts of the Holy Spirit as described in 1 Corinthians 12. This has helped the Church remain relevant and responsive to the evolving spiritual landscape in Nigeria. Additionally, the Church's emphasis on theological education and the formation of the laity has empowered more Nigerians to take active roles in their faith communities, bridging the gap between traditional practices and contemporary Christian living.

In conclusion, the cultural and religious diversity of Nigeria presents both challenges and opportunities for the Catholic Church. By engaging in respectful dialogue, the Church builds bridges with other faiths, fostering mutual understanding and peace. Embracing inculturation allows the Church to integrate Nigerian cultural elements into her practices, making the faith more accessible and meaningful to local communities. Meeting social needs through education, health, and social services demonstrates the Church's commitment to the well-being of all Nigerians and reflects Jesus' teachings about loving and serving others (Matthew 22:39).

Integrating traditional faith and Christian teachings enriches the faith experience of many Nigerians. It fosters a more inclusive and dynamic expression of the Catholic faith that respects both the past and the present. This approach will ensure that the Catholic Church remains an important and relevant institution capable of meeting the spiritual and social needs of the diverse population in Nigeria.

The Socio-Political Landscape

The socio-political environment in Nigeria significantly impacts religious practices, shaping how faith communities navigate their spiritual lives amidst evolving political dynamics. Nigeria, Africa's most populous country, is characterised by a complex interplay of ethnic, tribal, religious, and political factors that influence its socio-political landscape. Understanding this interplay is crucial for comprehending how the Catholic Church and other religious institutions operate within the country, how they are influenced, their recorded successes and failures, and their prospects for the future.

From a historical background, Nigeria's political environment has been tumultuous, marked by military coups, civil war, and periods of democratic governance. The legacy of colonialism, with its arbitrary borders and centralised political systems, has left a lasting impact on Nigeria's socio-political structure. These historical factors continue to influence contemporary political dynamics, affecting how religious communities, including the Catholic Church, engage with the state and society (Falola & Heaton, 2008).

One significant socio-political challenge affecting religious practices in Nigeria is the persistent ethno-religious conflict. Regions such as the Middle Belt have experienced frequent clashes between different ethnic and religious groups, often fueled by competition for resources and political power. These conflicts have led to significant loss of life and displacement of communities, impacting the ability of religious institutions to provide spiritual and social support (Osaghae & Suberu, 2005).

The Boko Haram insurgency in northeastern Nigeria is another profound example of how the socio-political landscape affects religious practices. Boko Haram, an Islamist militant group, continues to target Christians and moderate Muslims as they seek to establish an Islamic state. The group's violent activities, including bombings, kidnappings, and mass killings, have disrupted religious practices and forced many Christians to flee their homes. The Catholic Church, alongside other religious organisations, have been at the forefront of providing humanitarian aid and advocating for peace and reconciliation in affected regions (Agbiboa, 2013).

In response to these challenges, the Catholic Church in Nigeria has engaged in various socio-political activities aimed at promoting peace and justice. The Church's social teachings, as articulated in documents like *Gaudium et Spes and Evangelii Gaudium,* emphasise the importance of social justice, human dignity, and the common good. These teachings guide the Church's involvement in socio-political issues, encouraging clergy and laypeople to work towards a more just and peaceful society (Gaudium et Spes, 1965; Evangelii Gaudium, 2013).

The Catholic Church has also played a pivotal role in promoting democracy and good governance in Nigeria. During the military regimes of the late 20th century, Catholic leaders were vocal critics of military rule, advocating for a return to democratic governance. The Church's advocacy contributed to the eventual transition to democracy in 1999. In contemporary Nigeria, the Church continues to monitor elections, advocate for human rights, and hold government officials accountable, thereby strengthening democratic institutions (Ilesanmi, 1995).

Biblical references play a crucial role in guiding the Church's response to socio-political challenges. For instance, the call to *"seek justice, encourage the oppressed"* (Isaiah 1:17) underpins the Church's advocacy for social justice and human rights. Additionally, the Beatitudes, particularly *"Blessed are the peacemakers, for they will be called children of God"* (Matthew 5:9), inspire the Church's efforts in peacebuilding and reconciliation.

The socio-political landscape in Nigeria presents both challenges and opportunities for religious practices, particularly within the Catholic Church. By engaging with socio-political issues, promoting peace and justice, and addressing the needs of the oppressed, the Church navigates this complex environment effectively. Integrating biblical teaching and social action will enrich the faith experience of many Nigerians and promote a more inclusive and dynamic expression of the Catholic faith that is responsive to the socio-political realities of contemporary Nigeria.

Contemporary Nigeria is grappling with issues such as political instability, corruption, and insecurity, which have a profound impact on the Church's mission and witness (Ukah, 2012). The Church faces challenges in promoting social justice, human rights, and dignity, particularly in the face of violence, discrimination, and marginalisation (Catholic Bishops' Conference of Nigeria, 2017).

The entire Christian faith, particularly the Catholic Church in Nigeria, operates in a complex and dynamic socio-political space that is marked by significant challenges and opportunities (Catholic Bishops' Conference of Nigeria, 2017). Pope Francis noted, "The Church in Nigeria is called to be a prophetic voice in the midst of a society facing numerous challenges" (Pope Francis, 2015). Archbishop Ignatius Kaigama observed, "The

Church in Nigeria is not just a spiritual institution but a social and cultural force that shapes the nation's values and morals" (Kaigama, 2018). The Church's commitment to social justice and integral human development is crucial in addressing the socio-political challenges facing Nigeria (Ukah, 2012).

CHAPTER II

Navigating Faith and Culture

For many Nigerian Catholics, navigating the intersection of faith and culture is a personal journey of balancing traditional values with modern realities. This dynamic is particularly evident among the youths, who strive to maintain their Catholic identity amidst a rapidly changing cultural landscape influenced by globalisation and technological advancement.

In my own experience, growing up in a Catholic household in Nigeria meant participating in both Church and cultural festivals such as the *Egbe Festival* of the Egume people of Kogi State, dancing the *'Ogba'* dance when and where necessary, and learning to appreciate the richness of my heritage while embracing the universal values of the Catholic faith. This dual identity has fostered a deeper understanding of what it means to live out one's faith authentically in a diverse world without syncretism.

The introduction of Catholicism to Nigeria dates back to the 15th century, with the arrival of Portuguese missionaries. However, it wasn't until the 19th century, with the establishment of more permanent missions by the French Holy Ghost Fathers and later the Irish missionaries, that Catholicism began to take a firm root in Nigerian soil (Onaiyekan, 2004). These early missions laid the foundation for the growth of the Catholic Church, emphasising education, healthcare, and social services, which have become hallmarks of the Church's presence in Nigeria.

Catholicism in Nigeria is characterised by its efforts to harmonise Christian teachings with indigenous traditions. The Second Vatican Council's decree *Ad Gentes* emphasised the importance of inculturation, urging the Church to respect and incorporate local cultures into her liturgical and pastoral practices (Vatican II, 1965). This directive has been pivotal in Nigeria, where the Church has sought to embrace and uplift local customs while maintaining doctrinal integrity.

The use of native languages in the Mass and the adaptation of certain local rituals into Christian practices reflect this integration. Pope John Paul II highlighted during his visit to Nigeria that "The Church must become truly rooted in the local culture" (John Paul II, 1998).

Practicing Catholicism in Nigeria presents unique challenges and opportunities. The nation's rich cultural diversity often intersects with religious practices, creating a dynamic environment for faith expression.

Living out our faith and culture in Nigeria is challenging. A plurality of beliefs and occasional tensions between different religious groups mark the country's religious landscape. The Catholic Church often finds herself in a mediating role, advocating for peace and dialogue. The Nigerian Bishops' Conference frequently emphasises the need for religious tolerance and understanding, recognising the diverse religious fabric of the nation (CBCN, 2017).

Additionally, the Church faces the challenge of addressing contemporary social issues while staying true to her teachings. Topics such as gender equality, social justice, and political corruption are areas where the Church's voice is both influential and scrutinised. The Church's social teachings, as articulated in documents like *Gaudium et Spes*, call for active participation in the pursuit of justice and the common good, urging Nigerian Catholics to be agents of change in their society (Vatican II, 1965).

However, the relationship between faith and culture within Nigerian Catholicism is commendable and noteworthy. It is a testament to the Church's adaptability and commitment to inculturation. By valuing and integrating local traditions, the Catholic Church in Nigeria not only enriches her spiritual life but also strengthens her mission of evangelization and social transformation. As the Church continues to manoeuvre through this complex interplay, it remains a beacon of hope and unity in a country marked by its diversity.

Faith in a Multicultural Society

Living as a Catholic in Nigeria's multicultural environment means embracing a faith that is both universal and intimately connected to local traditions. For me, this means appreciating the beauty and depth of Nigerian culture while also being grounded in the teachings of the Catholic Church. It involves participating in vibrant liturgical celebrations that incorporate traditional elements and engaging in dialogues that foster mutual understanding and respect among different cultural and religious communities.

In a world where cultural and religious differences often lead to division, the Nigerian experience offers a hopeful model of how faith can bridge the gap and foster a more inclusive and harmonious society. The Catholic Church's engagement with a multicultural society like Nigeria exemplifies her commitment to inculturation, unity, and social justice. By embracing and celebrating cultural diversity, the Church not only enriches her spiritual life but also strengthens her mission of evangelization and social transformation.

Living out one's faith in a multicultural society like Nigeria also involves addressing contemporary social issues from a Catholic perspective, as articulated in *Gaudium et Spes*, which emphasise the importance of human dignity, social justice, and the common good (Vatican II, 1965). In Nigeria, these teachings inspire many Catholics to engage actively in social and political spheres, advocating for justice, human rights, and the eradication of corruption. For example, Catholic organisations and lay movements are often at the forefront of efforts to provide education, healthcare, and social services to underserved communities, embodying the Church's commitment to service and social transformation.

The understanding is to enculturate the Gospel message with local cultures while respecting and elevating Indigenous traditions. This principle was strongly emphasised in the Second Vatican Council's document *Ad Gentes*, which calls for the Church to "immerse herself in the cultural milieu of the people" (Vatican II, 1965). In Nigeria, this has translated into a rich synthesis where traditional music, dance, and attire are incorporated into liturgical celebrations, creating a deeply resonant and authentic worship experience.

The Catholic Church's universal nature finds a unique expression in Nigeria's multicultural setting. Pope Francis noted, "Diversity is not a threat but richness" (Francis, 2013). This perspective is essential in a country where over 250 ethnic groups coexist. The Church's mission in Nigeria often involves fostering unity and promoting a sense of community among these diverse groups, reflecting the Pauline vision of the Church as one body with many parts (1 Corinthians 12:12–27).

The Nigerian Catholic Bishops' Conference (CBCN) has been vocal in promoting unity amidst diversity, advocating for peaceful coexistence and mutual respect among different ethnic and religious groups (CBCN, 2017). This advocacy is crucial in addressing and mitigating inter-ethnic and inter-religious tensions that occasionally arise in the country.

Problems of Religious Life in a Multicultural Environment

The problems of religious life in a multicultural environment are complex and multifaceted. For the Catholic Church in Nigeria, addressing these issues involves a commitment to inculturation, inter-religious dialogue, and the promotion of religious freedom. Through these efforts, the Church not only confronts the challenges of multiculturalism but also celebrates and enhances the richness that such diversity brings to the faith experience. As a Nigerian Catholic, living a religious life in a multicultural environment means embracing both the challenges and the beauty of diversity. It involves actively participating in inter-religious dialogues, advocating for religious freedom, and contributing to the unity and growth of the Church. Nigeria's cultural diversity offers a unique perspective on what it means to live out the Catholic faith in a diverse environment, greatly enriching personal experiences of faith.

Living a religious life in a multicultural environment presents unique challenges and opportunities. For the Catholic Church, these challenges are navigated with a commitment to the principles of inculturation, unity, and dialogue. In a country like Nigeria, where cultural diversity is both a strength and a source of tension, the Catholic Church plays a crucial role in addressing the problems that arise from this complex interplay.

Inculturation

The Catholic Church's principle of inculturation, as emphasised in the Second Vatican Council's decree *Ad Gentes,* calls for the integration of the Gospel with local cultures (Vatican II, 1965). While this approach enriches the faith experience by making it more relevant to local contexts, it also poses significant challenges. One major issue is the potential for syncretism, where the blending of Christian and indigenous beliefs may lead to theological confusion or dilution of core Christian doctrines.

The difficulty of inculturation is apparent in Nigeria, as evidenced by the Catholic faith. In Nigeria, this challenge is particularly pronounced as the Church strives to respect and incorporate elements of diverse cultural traditions into its liturgy and practices without compromising the integrity of her faith. This delicate balance requires careful discernment and continuous education of both clergy and laity to ensure that cultural expressions enhance rather than undermine the Gospel message.

Inter-Religious Tensions

Nigeria's religious landscape is characterised by a diversity of beliefs, encompassing traditional African faiths, Islam, and Christianity. Despite being a source of cultural richness, this diversity frequently causes tensions and conflicts between different religions. The Catholic Church, advocating for peace and dialogue, frequently finds herself in a mediating role, striving to foster mutual understanding and respect among different religious groups.

The Nigerian Bishops' Conference (CBCN) has consistently emphasised the importance of inter-religious dialogue. In their pastoral letters, the bishops call for Catholics to engage with followers of other religions in a spirit of openness and respect, highlighting the need for collaborative efforts to address common social issues such as poverty, corruption, and violence (CBCN, 2017).

Embracing a new faith in a culturally diverse society like Nigeria comes with its own challenges. The country is home to more than 250 ethnic groups, each with its own unique language, customs, and religious practices. This diversity often results in complex interactions between different belief systems. One serious problem is religious pluralism. Nigerian society is a mix of Christians, Muslims, and followers of traditional African religions. This religious diversity can sometimes lead to tension and conflict, as seen in many parts of the country. For example, the Middle Belt region has experienced conflict rooted in ethnic and religious differences (Falola & Heaton, 2008). Such conflicts create an atmosphere of distrust and hostility, making it difficult for people to practice their faith freely and openly. Syncretism is also a major problem; this occurs when traditional beliefs are combined with Christian practices. Such mixing can enrich the religious experience, but it can also lead to confusion and theological debate within the Church. Some Catholics may incorporate traditional rituals and beliefs into Christian practices, which may sometimes conflict with Catholic teachings. This syncretism requires careful pastoral leadership to ensure that cultural expressions are respected while also respecting the fundamental principles of the faith.

Religious Freedom and Persecution

Another significant problem of religious life in a multicultural environment is the issue of religious freedom. In many parts of Nigeria, Christians face persecution and discrimination, particularly in regions where Islamic Sharia law is enforced. This situation poses a severe threat to the practice of faith and the safety of believers.

Pope Francis, in his apostolic exhortation *Evangelii Gaudium*, underscores the importance of religious freedom as a fundamental human right, stating that "a healthy pluralism... does not entail privatising religions in an attempt to reduce them to the quiet obscurity of the individual's conscience or relegate them to the enclosed precincts of churches, synagogues or mosques" (Francis, 2013). For Nigerian Catholics, advocating for religious freedom is a vital part of their witness in a multicultural society.

Internal Challenges within the Church

Multiculturalism can sometimes lead to internal divisions within the Catholic Church herself. In parishes and churches within the Federal Capital Territory, for instance, you find regional groupings such as Edo/Delta, Arewa, Igala, and Idoma. Even within people of the same region, we find further stratifications: Imo/Abia, Enugu, Anambra, Ebonyi Catholic communities, etc.

Differences in cultural backgrounds and traditions can create misunderstandings and conflicts among the faithful. Ensuring unity within such a diverse community requires strong pastoral leadership and effective communication. The Church and her Priests and pastors must work continuously to build bridges among her members, fostering a sense of belonging and mutual respect.

The Second Vatican Council's *Gaudium et Spes* speaks of the Church's role in promoting unity and peace in the world, asserting, "The Church, by reason of her role and competence, is not identified in any way with the political community nor bound to any political system. She is at once the sign and the safeguard of the transcendental dimension of the human person" (Vatican II, 1965). This teaching guides the Church in Nigeria as it seeks to unify her diverse membership while respecting the individuality of different cultural expressions.

Finally, the impact of modernisation and globalisation poses a challenge to preserving traditional religious values. The rapid spread of information and cultural exchange through media and technology exposes Nigerian society to a wide array of beliefs and lifestyles. This can lead to the dilution of religious practices and the adoption of secular values, particularly among the younger generation. The Catholic Church must find ways to engage with modernity while preserving her doctrinal integrity.

Opportunities for Witnessing to Faith in a Multicultural Setting

The diverse makeup of Nigerian society presents many opportunities for the Catholic religion to spread and thrive despite these obstacles. The rich cultures provide fertile ground for inculturation, where the Gospel can be expressed through local cultural forms. The *Church Constitution* document of the Second Vatican Council emphasises the importance of interaction with different cultures. "The Church educates and adopts, within good limits, the abilities, resources and customs of each people. It purifies, strengthens and uplifts them" (Lumen Gentium, 1964).

Living out one's faith in a multicultural environment like Nigeria offers special chances for development, enrichment, and deep interaction with various communities. Multiculturalism provides the Catholic Church, with her global mission, with a rich soil for social harmony and spiritual growth. Practising faith in a multicultural setting strengthens community bonds. The Catholic Church's emphasis on community and solidarity is especially relevant in diverse environments where fostering unity is essential. The Church provides a space where individuals from different cultural backgrounds can come together in worship and fellowship, creating a sense of unity and belonging.

The Nigerian Catholic community exemplifies this through her various communal activities, such as parish feasts, community service projects, and social justice initiatives. These activities bring people together, fostering a spirit of cooperation and mutual support. They also provide a platform for addressing common challenges such as poverty, inequality, and social injustice, thereby strengthening the social fabric of the community.

For individuals, practising the Christian faith in a multicultural setting offers significant opportunities for personal spiritual growth. Encountering different cultural expressions of faith can deepen one's understanding and appreciation of the Catholic faith. It encourages individuals to be more open, empathetic, and compassionate towards others, reflecting the universal love of Christ. Engaging with diverse cultural practices and perspectives challenges individuals to grow beyond their own cultural assumptions and biases. It fosters a broader worldview, enriching their spiritual journey. Pope Francis stated, "We are enriched by taking in what is different. Diversity is not a threat but a treasure" (Francis, 2013).

One of the important opportunities is the potential for interreligious dialogue. Nigeria's religious diversity provides a platform for meaningful dialogue between different faith communities. Such dialogue can promote mutual understanding, respect, and peace. The Church's commitment to dialogue is emphasised in the book *Nostra Aetate.* The book urges the Church to interact with people of other religions in a spirit of respect and cooperation (Nostra Aetate, 1965). Catholic leaders in Nigeria are actively involved in initiatives to promote interreligious harmony and address common social problems.

Opportunities for Evangelization

Multicultural settings provide a unique platform for evangelization. The diversity of cultures presents numerous opportunities to witness to the Gospel in ways that are respectful and resonant with different cultural contexts. The Second Vatican Council's decree *Ad Gentes* underscores the importance of proclaiming the Gospel to all peoples, adapting the message to the cultural context while preserving its core truths (Vatican II, 1965).

In Nigeria, the Catholic Church leverages cultural festivals, social events, and community gatherings as opportunities for evangelization. By participating in and contributing to these cultural activities, the Church can share the message of Christ in a way that is both meaningful and relevant to the local communities. This approach not only spreads the Gospel but also demonstrates the Church's respect and appreciation for local cultures.

Enrichment Through Diversity

One of the most significant opportunities for practising faith in a multicultural setting is the enrichment that comes from engaging with diverse cultures. The Second Vatican Council's document *Gaudium et Spes* emphasises that "the Church, by reason of her universal mission, is not committed to any one culture or to any political, economic, or social system" (Vatican II, 1965). This universality allows the Church to embrace and celebrate cultural diversity as a reflection of God's creative genius.

In Nigeria, the Catholic Church incorporates various cultural elements into her liturgical celebrations, making them more vibrant and relatable to the local populace. Traditional music, dance, attire, and languages are integrated into the Mass, creating a rich tapestry of worship that reflects the diverse heritage of the Nigerian people. This cultural integration not only enhances the worship experience but also fosters a deeper sense of belonging among the faithful.

Enrichment of the Church's Liturgy and Liturgical practices

The multicultural environment also allows for the enrichment of liturgical practice. By incorporating indigenous music, dance, and art into worship, churches can create a more inclusive and vibrant worship experience. This process of inculturation helps make the faith more accessible and understandable to local people. For example, in some Nigerian parishes, traditional drumming and singing are integral parts of the Mass, reflecting the cultural heritage of the congregation while celebrating the universality of the Catholic faith.

Furthermore, the Catholic Church's emphasis on social justice and community development resonates deeply in a multicultural society like Nigeria. The Church's social teachings, as articulated in documents such as *Gaudium et Spes* and *Caritas in Veritate*, underscore the importance of addressing social inequalities and promoting the common good. In Nigeria, the Church's involvement in education, healthcare, and social services has made significant contributions to the well-being of diverse communities. These efforts not only address immediate needs but also build bridges between different cultural and religious groups, fostering a sense of unity and solidarity.

Fostering Intercultural Dialogue

A multicultural environment offers the opportunity for meaningful intercultural dialogue. The Catholic Church, with her emphasis on dialogue and understanding, plays a pivotal role in facilitating conversations between different cultural and religious groups. Pope Francis, in his encyclical *Fratelli Tutti,* highlights the importance of dialogue, stating, "It calls for perseverance; it entails moments of silence, suffering and patience; it can patiently embrace the broader experience of individuals and peoples" (Francis, 2020).

In Nigeria, where cultural and religious diversity is prominent, the Church actively promotes dialogue through various interfaith and intercultural initiatives. These efforts help to promote understanding, reduce prejudices, and promote peace and harmony in society. Engaging in dialogue with people of different cultural backgrounds also enriches the Church's understanding of humanity and God's creation.

Strengthening Community Bonds

Practising faith in a multicultural setting strengthens community bonds. The Catholic Church's emphasis on community and solidarity is especially relevant in diverse environments where fostering unity is essential. The Church provides a space where individuals from different cultural backgrounds can come together in worship and fellowship, creating a sense of unity and belonging.

The Nigerian Catholic community exemplifies this through her various communal activities, such as parish feasts, community service projects, and social justice initiatives. These activities bring people together, fostering a spirit of cooperation and mutual support. They also provide a platform for addressing common challenges such as poverty, inequality, and social injustice, thereby strengthening the social fabric of the community.

In conclusion, the opportunities for practising faith in a multicultural setting are manifold and profoundly enriching. For the Catholic Church in Nigeria, these opportunities include cultural enrichment, fostering dialogue, evangelization, strengthening community bonds, and personal spiritual growth. By embracing and celebrating cultural diversity, the Church not only enhances her own mission but also contributes to the broader goals of peace, understanding, and social harmony.

The Role of Catholic Priests and Religious

As a Catholic Priest with my unique experience and also someone who has experienced the ministry of Catholic Priests in Nigeria, I have firsthand knowledge of the impact of committed service. Whether through compassionate pastoral care, efforts to integrate cultural traditions into worship, commitment to education, advocacy for justice, or engagement in inter-religious dialogue, Priests play a pivotal role in nurturing the faith and well-being of their communities. The role of Catholic Priests in a multicultural society like Nigeria is both challenging and rewarding. By serving as spiritual leaders, promoters of inculturation, educators, advocates for social justice, and facilitators of dialogue, Priests help to navigate the complexities of cultural diversity while fostering a vibrant and inclusive faith community. Their work is essential in building a Church that genuinely reflects the universality of the Catholic faith and the richness of human diversity.

Spiritual Leadership and Pastoral Care

Catholic Priests are primarily spiritual leaders tasked with guiding the faithful in their journey towards holiness. According to the Second Vatican Council's *Presbyterorum Ordinis*, Priests are called to "serve the people of God in a way that promotes unity, charity, and peace" (Vatican II, 1965). In a multicultural setting like Nigeria, this role involves addressing the diverse spiritual needs of parishioners who come from various ethnic and cultural backgrounds. Priests provide pastoral care through the administration of the sacraments, including the Eucharist, confession, and anointing of the sick. They offer spiritual counselling and support, helping individuals and families through life's challenges. Also, by fostering a welcoming and inclusive parish environment, Priests play a crucial role in uniting diverse communities under the banner of faith.

Facilitators of Inter-Religious Dialogue

In a multicultural society marked by religious diversity, Catholic Priests play a significant role in facilitating inter-religious dialogue. The Church's commitment to dialogue with other faiths is articulated in documents like *Nostra Aetate*, which calls for respect and collaboration between people of different religions (Vatican II, 1965).

Priests in Nigeria often engage with leaders and followers of other religious traditions, fostering mutual understanding and cooperation. They participate in interfaith forums, promote peacebuilding initiatives, and work to resolve conflicts that arise from religious differences. Through these efforts, Priests help to bridge the gap between communities and promote social harmony.

Advocates for Social Justice

Catholic Priests are called to be advocates for social justice, addressing the social and economic challenges facing their communities. This aspect of their role is grounded in the Church's social teaching, which emphasises the preferential option for the poor and the pursuit of justice and peace (Gaudium et Spes, 1965). In Nigeria, Priests often engage in social justice initiatives, such as providing aid to the poor, advocating for human rights, and addressing issues like corruption and violence. They work alongside lay organisations and community leaders to promote the common good and uplift marginalised populations, and by doing so, they embody the Church's mission to be a force for positive change in society.

Subsequently, as Priests engage in interreligious dialogue, they build relationships with leaders of other faith communities, which helps create opportunities for collaboration on social issues and the promotion of peace and reconciliation. This requires a deep commitment to the principles of respect, understanding, and cooperation enshrined in *Nostra Aetate.*

Additionally, Priests are asked to address socio-political issues that affect their communities. This includes advocating for justice, peace and human rights, as well as providing pastoral care to people affected by conflict and violence. The prophetic voice of the Church, spoken by priests, can be a powerful force for social change and for promoting the common good.

Educators and Catechists

Education is another critical aspect of a priest's role. Priests are responsible for educating their parishioners on the faith shared, ensuring that they understand Catholic doctrine and are able to live out their beliefs in daily life. This role is highlighted in the

Catechism of the Catholic Church, which states, "The pastoral duty of Priests is to ensure that the faithful are properly instructed" (Catechism of the Catholic Church, 1992). In Nigeria, Priests often oversee catechism classes, Bible study groups, and adult faith formation programs. They also play a key role in the administration of Catholic schools, where they help to shape the moral and spiritual education of young people. By promoting a well-rounded education that integrates faith with academic excellence, Priests contribute to the holistic development of individuals and communities.

In a multicultural environment, Priests must be culturally sensitive and aware of the diverse backgrounds of their parishioners. This involves understanding local customs, language and traditions and finding ways to incorporate them into religious practice without compromising Catholic doctrine. For example, a Priest might incorporate traditional storytelling into his sermon or encourage a local choir to participate in the service. A priest's pastoral approach must be flexible, sensitive and based on the teachings of the Church.

Promoters of Inculturation

In Nigeria's multicultural context, Catholic Priests are instrumental in promoting inculturation - the process of integrating the Gospel message with local cultures. The Church's commitment to inculturation is rooted in the teachings of the Second Vatican Council's decree *Ad Gentes,* which encourages the adaptation of Christian teachings to different cultural contexts (Vatican II, 1965). Priests facilitate this process by incorporating local traditions, languages, and customs into liturgical celebrations. This might include using indigenous music, dance, and art in worship, thereby making the liturgy more relatable and meaningful to the local community. Through such efforts, Priests help the Church to be truly universal while respecting and valuing cultural diversity.

Pope John Paul II further articulated this vision in his encyclical *Redemptoris Missio*, highlighting the need for the Gospel to be incarnated in various cultural forms. He wrote, "The process of the Church's insertion into peoples' cultures is a lengthy one. It is not limited to adaptation, but takes the form of a profound and all-encompassing process, which takes time to unfold" (John Paul II, 1990).

The challenges and opportunities of practising faith in a multicultural society are deeply rooted in biblical and theological principles. Scripture provides numerous examples of cultural diversity and calls for its use in the practice of faith. The story of Pentecost in Acts 2:1-12 demonstrates the universality of the Gospel and its embrace of people from diverse cultures. The ability of the apostles to speak multiple languages symbolises the Church's mission to spread the message of Christ to all peoples and cultures.

The theological concept of the Body of Christ expressed in 1 Corinthians 12:12-27 emphasises unity and diversity within the Church. Just as the body is made up of many members with different functions, the Church is made up of many different parts that contribute to the overall mission of the Church. This diversity is not a barrier but a force that allows the Church to reflect the Kingdom of God.

The teachings of the Church reflected in documents such as *Lumen Gentium* and *Gaudium et Spes*, provide the basis for managing faith in a multicultural society. These documents emphasise the Church's mission to engage with the world, promote social justice, and respect cultural diversity. They call for a pastoral approach that is inclusive, compassionate and gospel-centered.

In conclusion, practising faith in a multicultural society like Nigeria presents both significant challenges and tremendous opportunities. The Catholic Church has the potential to effectively manage this difficult situation based on her biblical and theological foundations. By engaging in respectful dialogue and inculturation and meeting societal needs, the Church can promote more inclusive and dynamic expressions of Catholicism. Catholic Priests play a critical role in this effort as they lead their communities in culturally sensitive ways, foster interreligious dialogue, and advocate for social justice. Through these efforts, the Catholic Church in Nigeria can faithfully proclaim the universal message of Christ while respecting its rich cultural heritage.

Integrating Traditional Beliefs and Catholic Doctrine

The integration of traditional beliefs with Catholic doctrine is a dynamic and delicate process, particularly in multicultural societies like Nigeria. This practice, known as inculturation, seeks to make the Gospel message relevant to local cultures while preserving the integrity of Catholic teachings.

Inculturation is deeply rooted in the Catholic Church's understanding of the universality of the Gospel and her mission to evangelize to all nations. The Second Vatican Council's decree *Ad Gentes* emphasises the importance of adapting the Christian message to different cultural contexts. It states, "The Church must be inserted into the native culture, and in turn, that culture must be permeated by the Gospel" (Vatican II, 1965). This mutual enrichment allows the faith to take root in diverse cultural settings.

As a Nigerian Catholic, witnessing the integration of traditional beliefs with Catholic doctrine has been profoundly enriching.

It demonstrates the Church's respect for cultural diversity and her commitment to making the faith accessible and relevant to all people. Through this process, I have seen how the universal message of the Gospel can be expressed in diverse ways, deepening our collective understanding of God's love and presence in our lives.

Integrating traditional beliefs with Catholic doctrine in a multicultural setting like Nigeria is a complex but rewarding endeavour. By embracing the principles of inculturation, the Church can enrich her liturgy, deepen spirituality, foster evangelization, and promote social justice. While challenges remain, the opportunities for growth and mutual enrichment are vast, allowing the Church to truly embody her universal mission.

The dynamic interplay between traditional beliefs and Catholic doctrine in Nigeria offers both challenges and opportunities for the Church. This integration is not only about preserving cultural heritage but also about enriching the faith experience of the Catholic community. By examining specific examples, drawing on personal experiences, and interviewing priests, we will gain a deeper understanding of how this fusion contributes to a more inclusive and vibrant expression of Catholicism in Nigeria.

Examples of Integration

One significant example of integrating traditional beliefs with Catholic teachings is the use of indigenous music and dance in liturgical celebrations. In many Nigerian parishes, traditional drumming, singing, and dancing are integral parts of the Mass. These cultural expressions bring a sense of joy and communal participation that is deeply meaningful to the congregation. This practice aligns with the Second Vatican Council's *Sacrosanctum Concilium*, which encourages the incorporation of cultural elements into worship. "The Church fosters and takes to herself, in so far as they are good, the ability, resources, and customs of each people" (Sacrosanctum Concilium, 1963).

Another example is celebrating local holidays as part of Catholic holidays. For example, some communities combine traditional harvest festivals with the Feast of St. Michael, celebrating both the Archangel and the local agricultural cycle. This blend of traditions allows believers to respect their cultural heritage and be grateful for God's blessings. The Church recognises that such practices can deepen the spiritual life of the faithful by bringing the liturgy closer to their daily lives.

It is also common to incorporate traditional symbols and rituals into Catholic practices. For example, in the Yoruba culture, the use of kola nuts in ceremonies symbolises hospitality and blessing. Some Catholic Priests have adapted this practice by incorporating the blessing and sharing of kola nuts into the liturgy, particularly during special occasions like weddings and community celebrations. This practice not only respects cultural customs but also enriches the sacramental life of the Church. It reflects the Church's understanding, as articulated in *Lumen Gentium*, "The Church, sent to all peoples of every time and place, is not tied exclusively and indissolubly to any race or nation, to any customary way of life, ancient or recent" (Lumen Gentium, 1964).

Personal Experiences and Interviews

Father Emmanuel, a Priest in the Archdiocese of Lagos, shared his experience of integrating traditional beliefs with Catholic doctrine. He explained how the first yam is blessed in the Church before being distributed to the community during the annual yam festival. This blessing ceremony is an affirmation of God's providence and is a powerful way to connect local agricultural traditions with faith. Fr. Emmanuel explained it this way: "By blessing the yams, we remind the community that all good things come from God and that their labour cooperates with God's grace."

Father Patrick, from the Diocese of Onitsha, highlighted the importance of storytelling in his ministry. In Igbo culture, storytelling is a vital means of preserving history and teaching moral lessons. Father Patrick incorporates traditional stories into his homilies, drawing parallels between the stories and biblical teachings. He shared, "When I tell a traditional story that people know and love and then connect it to a Gospel message, it makes the faith more relatable and impactful." This method of teaching not only engages the congregation but also bridges the gap between cultural wisdom and Christian doctrine.

Father Anthony, serving in a rural parish in the Niger Delta, has integrated traditional healing practices with the sacrament of anointing of the sick. He observed that many parishioners held strong beliefs in the healing power of herbs and traditional medicine. To address this, Father Anthony invites local herbalists to bless the herbs used in these practices during a special Mass, combining the traditional belief in natural remedies with the Church's teaching on divine healing. He noted, "This approach helps the people see that their faith in God's healing power does not contradict their cultural practices but complements them."

Biblical and Theological Foundations

The integration of traditional beliefs with Catholic doctrine is deeply rooted in biblical and theological principles. Scripture supports the concept of inculturation, where the Gospel is seen as transcending cultural boundaries. In Acts 17:22–28, Paul's speech at the Areopagus demonstrates how he used the Athenians' religious beliefs to introduce them to the Gospel.

Similarly, the Catholic Church in Nigeria uses local cultural elements to deepen the faith experience of her members.

Theological support for this integration can also be found in *Lumen Gentium*, which states, "The Church, sent to all peoples of every time and place, is not tied exclusively and indissolubly to any race or nation, to any customary way of life, ancient or recent" (Lumen Gentium, 1964). This openness allows the Church to embrace cultural diversity and incorporate it into the practice of faith.

Furthermore, in *Nostra Aetate*, the declaration on the relationship of the Church with non-Christian religions highlights the importance of recognising and valuing elements of truth and holiness in other religions. It states, "The Catholic Church rejects nothing that is true and holy in these religions. She regards with sincere reverence those ways of conduct and life, those precepts and teachings which, though differing in many aspects from the ones she holds and sets forth, nonetheless often reflect a ray of that truth which enlightens all men." (Nostra Aetate, 1965). This perspective encourages the Church to engage with traditional beliefs and practices in a spirit of respect and mutual enrichment.

Summarily, the integration of traditional beliefs with Catholic doctrine in Nigeria is a testament to the Church's adaptability and respect for cultural diversity. Through examples like the incorporation of music, festivals, symbols, and storytelling, we see how local traditions can deeply enrich the Catholic faith. The personal experiences of Priests like Father Emmanuel, Father Patrick, and Father Anthony highlight the effectiveness of this integration in making the faith more accessible and meaningful to the Nigerian people. The Catholic Church in Nigeria honours cultural heritage while faithfully proclaiming the Gospel by embracing inculturation.

Case Studies of Cultural Integration

Integrating traditional beliefs with Catholic doctrine has been a dynamic and multifaceted process in Nigeria. Here, I will explore specific case studies showcasing successful cultural integration, highlighting how local traditions have been harmonised with Catholic teachings to create a unique expression of faith. Through these examples, one will gain insights into the practical aspects of cultural integration and its impact on the faith community.

Introduction to Cultural Integration

Cultural integration within the Catholic Church in Nigeria involves blending traditional African beliefs and practices with Catholic doctrine to create a harmonious and enriched faith experience. This process, known as inculturation, allows the Church to remain relevant and relatable to her diverse congregations. According to *Lumen Gentium*, the Church must respect and incorporate the cultural elements of the communities she serves as long as they align with Christian values (Second Vatican Council, 1964). This approach not only preserves cultural identity but also enhances the spiritual life of the faithful.

Case Study 1: The Aladura Movement

One notable example of cultural integration is the Aladura movement, which emerged in the early 20th century as a response to the perceived inadequacies of missionary-led churches. The Aladura movement, meaning "Owners of Prayer," integrates indigenous spiritual practices with Christian beliefs. This movement emphasises prayer, healing, and direct experiences of the Holy Spirit, reflecting a synthesis of traditional African spirituality and Christianity. For example, during worship, you can often see elements such as drumming, dancing, and the use of local languages that are deeply rooted in African culture. These practices resonate within the community, making faith experiences more meaningful and culturally relevant. The success of the Aladura movement in integrating these elements shows how traditional beliefs can coexist with Catholic doctrine to enrich the spiritual life of a community.

Case 2: Igbo Church Ceremony

The Igbo people of southeastern Nigeria have successfully integrated their cultural rituals with Catholic rituals. A representative example is the celebration of the Yam Festival, which marks the beginning of the harvest season. Traditionally, this festival includes ceremonies to thank the gods for a bountiful harvest and seek blessings for the coming year. In the Igbo Catholic community, the festival has been adapted to include a special mass where the Priest blesses and distributes yams to the congregation. This adaptation preserves the cultural significance of the festival while being consistent with Catholic teachings on gratitude and divine providence. By incorporating the New Yam festival into the church calendar, the Igbo Catholic community honours its cultural heritage and strengthens its faith.

Case Study 3: Yoruba Naming Ceremony

For the Yoruba people of southwestern Nigeria, naming ceremonies are an important cultural event. Traditionally, these rituals include prayers, blessings, and the use of symbolic objects to convey good wishes to the newborn. In the Yoruba Catholic community, these elements have been incorporated into the Church's Baptism ritual. In a Catholic naming ceremony, the Priest includes traditional prayers and blessings in the Baptism ceremony to ensure the cultural significance of the event is maintained. This integration not only strengthens the spiritual meaning of Baptism but also promotes a deeper connection between the community's cultural identity and the Catholic faith. As emphasised in *Nostra Aetate*, the Church strives to exploit and celebrate the positive aspects of local culture (Second Vatican Council, 1965).

Case Study 4: The Tiv Traditional Dances

In central Nigeria, the Tiv people are known for their rich cultural heritage, including traditional dances that play a vital role in their social and religious life. These dances, characterised by rhythmic movements and vibrant costumes, are often performed during significant events and celebrations.

In Tiv Catholic communities, traditional dances have been integrated into Church celebrations, particularly during feast days and special liturgical events. For example, during the Feast of St. Augustine, which is widely celebrated among the Tiv, traditional dances are performed as part of the procession and offertory. This integration not only preserves the cultural heritage of the Tiv people but also enhances the communal and celebratory aspects of the faith.

Personal Experiences and Insights

Interviews with Catholic Priests who have firsthand experience in this area are invaluable for gaining deeper insights into the process of cultural integration.

Father Emmanuel Okafor, a Priest serving in the Igbo region of Nigeria, shares his perspective, "Integrating traditional beliefs with Catholic teachings has been a journey of mutual enrichment. By embracing cultural practices, we create a more inclusive and relatable faith experience for our parishioners." He emphasises that cultural integration must be done with discernment, ensuring that the core tenets of Catholic doctrine are upheld.

He also notes that the process involves continuous dialogue and collaboration with local communities to identify practices that can be harmoniously incorporated into the Church's liturgy and teachings.

Father Michael Adewale from the Yoruba region reflects on the positive impact of cultural integration, stating, "By incorporating Yoruba customs into our religious ceremonies, we foster a sense of belonging and pride among our parishioners. It reinforces the idea that the Catholic faith is not foreign but deeply connected to our cultural identity."

Personal Reflections and Experiences

Serving faith and culture as a Catholic Priest in Nigeria has been a pathway filled with challenges and opportunities. Here, I will share my personal reflections and experiences, offering insights into how faith can be practised in a multicultural society. One can expect a candid exploration of the rewards and difficulties of integrating Catholic doctrine with traditional beliefs, grounded in real-life encounters and supported by theological reflections.

In a country as diverse as Nigeria, where multiple ethnic groups and religious traditions coexist, the role of a Catholic Priest extends beyond spiritual guidance to include being a bridge among different cultures. This message highlights the intersection of faith and culture. Through these reflections, I hope to provide insight into how Catholic Priests can address these issues while maintaining the integrity of their faith.

Embracing Cultural Diversity

One of the highlights of my ministry is observing the culture of our community. Each ethnic group has its own traditions, language and ways of expressing its beliefs. Embracing this diversity has not only enriched my own spiritual journey but also our communal worship experience.

For example, during the Feast of Pentecost, our parish celebrates a multicultural Mass where readings and prayers are offered in various local languages. Inspired by Acts 2:1–11, where the Holy Spirit gives the apostles the authority to speak in many languages, this practice symbolises the unity and diversity of the Church. A day of rest like this reminds us that the Holy Spirit works across our cultural differences to create more vibrant and inclusive faith communities.

The Problem of Cultural Integration

Despite the beauty of cultural diversity, integrating traditional beliefs and Catholic doctrine poses serious challenges. One of the notable challenges is dealing with issues that run counter to Catholic teachings. For example, some traditional healing practices and rituals that are deeply rooted in local culture may conflict with the Church's position on the Eucharist and Holy Communion.

In these situations, it is important to have respectful conversations with the community. I remember a case where a family wanted to perform a traditional purification ritual for a sick relative that included elements that did not conform to Catholic teachings. By discussing the importance of the anointing of the sick (James 5:14–15) and finding ways to integrate their cultural symbols into their sacramental practices, we reached a compromise that respected both their cultural heritage and Catholic doctrine.

Personal Growth Through Cultural Exchange

Exposure to different cultures has greatly contributed to my personal and spiritual growth. Each time I encountered traditional customs and beliefs, my understanding of how faith can be practised in different ways deepened. Through this involvement, I learned the importance of humility and openness in ministry.

One example is participating in the traditional New Yam festival with the Igbo community. This event honours the first harvest of yams and is a time for community harmony and thankfulness. As I participated in the festival and celebrated a special mass for the blessing of yams, I saw firsthand how cultural traditions can fit together with Catholic rituals. This integration not only deepened our connection to the community but also strengthened the biblical principle of being thankful for God's provision (Deuteronomy 16:9–12).

The Role of Dialogue and Education

Effective cultural integration requires ongoing dialogue and education. As a priest, it is very important for me to learn the cultural traditions of the communities I serve. This knowledge allows me to approach cultural integration with sensitivity and respect.

Our parish has created a cultural committee that includes representatives of different cultures. This committee plays an important advisory role on how to integrate cultural elements into liturgical celebrations. Through regular meetings and discussions, we developed a deeper understanding of each other's traditions, which enriched our shared worship and strengthened our bonds.

Theological Reflection

The teachings of the Second Vatican Council support cultural integration theologically. 'The Light of the Church emphasises the Church's mission in interaction with diverse cultures, saying, "All people are called to belong to the new people of God" (Second Vatican Council, 1964). This universal calling requires the Church to respect and integrate cultural elements consistent with Christian values.

Nostra Aetate once again emphasises the importance of mutual understanding and respect between different cultures and religions (Second Vatican Council, 1965). By recognising the positive aspects of local traditions, churches can build bridges and foster unity among their diverse members.

Lessons from Pastoral Ministry

My experience in pastoral ministry has taught me valuable lessons about cultural inclusion. First, it is important to approach cultural practices with an open mind and insight. Although not all traditions can be easily integrated into Catholic doctrine, many can be applied in ways that enrich the experience of faith.

Secondly, it is important to build strong relationships with community leaders and elders. Their support and guidance is critical to understanding cultural differences and building trust within the community. By involving them in decision-making, we can ensure that cultural integration is respected and inclusive.

Finally, ongoing education and training are important. Both Priests and laity need training on the importance of cultural integration and the theological foundations that support it. Such education helps eliminate misunderstandings and promotes more cohesive and vibrant faith communities.

Impact of Cultural Integration on Faith

Cultural integration has a profound impact on the religious life of a society. When traditional beliefs are harmonised with Catholic doctrine, a more understandable and meaningful worship experience is created. This integration fosters a sense of belonging and pride among believers and strengthens their cultural identity within the context of their faith.

Moreover, cultural unity strengthens the Church's mission of evangelization. By respecting and embracing cultural elements, the Church becomes more accessible to those who feel alienated from traditional Western Catholic beliefs. This approach is consistent with the Apostle Paul's principle of "becoming all things to all people" to spread the gospel effectively (1 Corinthians 9:22).

Exploring faith and culture as a Catholic Priest in Nigeria is a dynamic and enriching journey. Through personal experience and reflection, I have witnessed the beauty and challenges of cultural integration. By embracing cultural diversity, engaging in respectful dialogue, and working to build on theological principles, we can create a more inclusive and vibrant church.

The case studies and personal insights presented in this chapter highlight the importance of cultural inclusion in enhancing the experience of faith and strengthening the mission of the Church. As we continue to navigate this complex landscape, let us remain open to the transformative power of cultural diversity and the unifying presence of the Holy Spirit.

CHAPTER III

The Christian Faith and Political Participation in Nigeria

In Nigeria, neglecting the role of religion or religious belief in the political matrix is like moving on a slippery slope. The influence of religion on our politics in Nigeria is obvious as it influences virtually every phase of the nation's political and economic life, from who to vote or not vote into office to who gets what, when and how. It influences policy formulations and implementation as well. Grounded in the principles of her foundational documents, the Church continues to urge her faithful and clergy to engage in the political sphere conscientiously and morally.

The intersection of the Christian faith and political participation in Nigeria resonates deeply with me. It touches on the challenges faced by many Nigerians and their hope for a better society. The role of faith in guiding political actions and decisions is not just theoretical but lived out in the daily struggles and triumphs of people across the nation.

As a Nigerian, I have experienced the frustration and disillusionment that comes from seeing public resources mismanaged and leaders who prioritise personal gain over the common good. This situation calls for a profound moral and ethical reawakening that is grounded in the values of integrity and accountability. Nigeria's political landscape is often characterised by instability and corruption, which undermine the potential for genuine development and social justice. The Catholic Church in Nigeria has been vocal in advocating for transparency and good governance. The frequent pastoral letters and statements from the Catholic Bishops' Conference of Nigeria (CBCN) serve as moral compasses, guiding the faithful towards ethical political participation. This advocacy has empowered many Christians to demand better governance and to participate actively in democratic processes.

Catholic teachings emphasise the dignity of human life and the importance of social and economic justice, guiding the political actions and beliefs of its adherents. By promoting these values, the Church not only influences policies but also moulds the ethical framework within which political decisions are made, fostering a society more reflective of the Christian call to love and serve. During the colonial period, Christian missionaries played a critical role in the country's socio-political development, introducing Western education, healthcare, and social services that laid the foundation for the modern Nigerian state (Hastings, 1986).

Missionaries such as Bishop Shanahan and Reverend Hope Waddell were instrumental in establishing schools and hospitals, which not only evangelized but also provided essential services to the local population. This dual role of the Church in both spiritual and temporal matters established a template for future engagements with the state.

As Nigeria moved towards independence, religious leaders were at the forefront of the struggle for self-determination and justice (Igbafe, 1979). Figures like Cardinal Dominic Ekandem and Archbishop Anthony Olubunmi Okogie were vocal in their demands for an end to colonial rule and the establishment of a democratic government that respected human rights and dignity. Their involvement underscored the moral and ethical dimensions that faith brought to the political discourse of the time.

In the post-independence era, the Catholic Church has continued to advocate for social justice, human rights, and good governance (Catholic Bishops' Conference of Nigeria, 2020). During the military regimes, the Church often acted as a voice of conscience, condemning abuses of power and calling for a return to democratic governance. For instance, the pastoral letters issued by the Catholic Bishops' Conference of Nigeria (CBCN) during this period emphasised the need for justice, accountability, and the protection of human rights.

The Church's Role in Nigerian Politics

The Catholic Church in Nigeria has played a significant role in the political landscape, advocating for democracy, human rights, and social justice (Catholic Bishops' Conference of Nigeria, 2020). Through her teachings, pastoral letters, and public statements, the Church has addressed critical issues like corruption, electoral malpractices, and human rights abuses. The Church's leaders often speak out on political matters, calling for accountability, transparency, and good governance.

One notable example is the CBCN's statement on the 2019 general elections, which called for free, fair, and credible elections. The bishops condemned the use of violence, vote-buying, and other malpractices, urging politicians to respect the people's will. This advocacy is rooted in the Church's belief in the dignity of the human person and the right of individuals to participate in the political process.

The Church also engages in political education. Through her various institutions, such as schools and seminaries, the Church educates her members on their civic responsibilities and the importance of participating in the political process. This education is crucial for building an informed and active citizenry that can contribute to the democratic process. The Justice, Development and Peace Commission (JDPC), a social arm of the Church, has been instrumental in this regard, organising voter education programs and promoting civic engagement.

Additionally, the Church provides social services that address the root causes of political instability. By offering healthcare, education, and social welfare programs, the Church helps to alleviate poverty and inequality, which are often sources of political tension. These services not only meet immediate needs but also promote long-term social and political stability.

Social and Political Challenges

Despite her significant role, the Catholic Church faces several challenges when engaging with politics. One of the primary challenges is maintaining a balance between spiritual and political roles. The Church must navigate the delicate boundary between advocating for justice and being perceived as partisan. This balance is essential to maintain her moral authority and credibility. The Church's involvement in political issues must be seen as an extension of her mission to promote the common good rather than an alignment with any political party or ideology.

Another challenge is the risk of politicization of religion. In Nigeria, religion is often intertwined with ethnic and regional identities, which can lead to the manipulation of religious sentiments for political gain. The Church must remain vigilant against such manipulations and ensure that her engagement in politics is guided by principles of justice and the common good rather than partisan interests. The challenge is compounded by the diverse nature of the Nigerian Catholic community, which includes different ethnic groups with varying political affiliations.

Furthermore, the Church faces the challenge of addressing internal divisions. The diverse nature of the Nigerian Catholic community means that there are different perspectives on political issues. The Church must work towards fostering unity and ensuring that her political advocacy reflects the collective values and teachings of the faith. This requires careful discernment and dialogue within the Church to ensure that a broad consensus informs its positions and is consistent with her mission and teachings.

Christians in Nigeria face serious social and political challenges that affect their ministry and call to witnessing. Issues such as poverty, corruption and violence create an environment in which Priests must navigate complex situations every day. Priests often serve as advocates for justice and peace in accordance with biblical principles and church teachings. For example, Proverbs 31:8-9 exhorts believers to *"speak for those who cannot speak for themselves" and "stand up for the rights of the poor and needy."* This commitment is reinforced by the document *Lumen Gentium,* which calls for active participation in promoting the common good.

Growing up in Nigeria, I have witnessed firsthand the devastating effects of religious persecution and violence. Stories of churches being attacked and communities displaced are not just news headlines but lived realities for many Nigerians. These acts of violence are often perpetrated by extremist groups like Boko

Haram, who target Christians and other religious minorities. The fear and uncertainty that these attacks bring can be paralyzing.

However, amid this adversity, the resilience and faith of the Christian community have been a source of inspiration. I have seen Priests and lay leaders who, despite the threats, continue to provide spiritual and material support to their congregations. Their courage and commitment to peace and reconciliation embody the teachings of Christ and the Church's mission. It reminds me of the words of Pope Francis, who calls for active non-violence and peace-building as essential Christian duties (Francis, 2017).

Opportunities for the Church

Despite these challenges, there are significant opportunities for the Catholic Church to influence positive political change in Nigeria. One of the key opportunities is the potential for the Church to serve as a mediator in political conflicts. Given her moral authority and extensive network, the Church can play a crucial role in promoting dialogue and reconciliation among conflicting parties. This role is particularly important in a country like Nigeria, where political conflicts often have ethnic and religious dimensions.

The Church also has the opportunity to lead by example in promoting ethical leadership. By adhering to principles of transparency, accountability, and service in her own institutions, the Church can set a standard for political leaders to follow. This leadership, by example, can inspire trust and confidence in the Church's political advocacy. For instance, the transparent management of Church-run schools and hospitals can serve as a model for public institutions, demonstrating the benefits of ethical governance.

Additionally, the Church can leverage her global connections to advocate for international support for good governance in Nigeria. By collaborating with international Catholic organisations and other faith-based groups, the Church can amplify her voice and influence on the global stage, advocating for policies that promote justice and development in Nigeria. This international solidarity can provide additional pressure on the Nigerian government to adhere to democratic principles and respect human rights.

Practical Strategies for Political Engagement

To effectively manage the relationship between faith and politics, the Catholic Church in Nigeria can adopt several practical strategies that embody the Church's teachings and stance on socio-political issues.

Advocacy

Advocacy is a primary method through which Catholic Priests in Nigeria engage with political issues. Priests often use their platforms to speak out against corruption, electoral malpractices, and human rights abuses. This engagement is deeply rooted in the Church's social teachings, as outlined in documents like *Gaudium et Spes and Pacem in Terris. Gaudium et Spes* emphasise the Church's responsibility to promote social justice and human dignity, urging all Christians to participate in the construction of a just world (Gaudium et Spes., 1965). Similarly, *Pacem in Terris* highlights the importance of human rights and the necessity of establishing an order based on truth, justice, love, and freedom (Pacem in Terris, 1963).

Additionally, developing well-researched and evidence-based positions on political issues can help the Church effectively communicate her stance and influence public policy. For example, the Church can commission studies on issues like corruption, poverty, and healthcare and use the findings to advocate for policy reforms.

Community Organising

Another significant form of political engagement is community organising. Priests work closely with local communities to address pressing socio-political issues such as poverty, healthcare, and education. This approach is informed by the Church's call to action in documents like *Octogesima Adveniens*, which emphasises the need for Christians to engage in social issues and take concrete action to promote social justice (Octogesima Adveniens, 1971).

Through community organising, Priests empower community members to take collective action and advocate for their rights. This involves creating awareness about social issues, facilitating discussions, and helping communities develop strategies to address their concerns. For instance, Priests may organise workshops on health and education, bringing together experts and community members to discuss solutions and advocate for better services. By fostering a sense of solidarity and collective responsibility, Priests help communities become more resilient and proactive in demanding change from political leaders.

A biblical basis for this engagement can be found in the teachings of the prophets, who frequently called for social justice and care for the marginalised. Isaiah 1:17 urges, "*Learn to do right; seek justice. Defend the oppressed. Take up the cause of the fatherless; plead the case of the widow.*" This scriptural mandate encourages Priests to work towards creating a more just society, aligning their efforts with the prophetic tradition of advocating for the vulnerable.

In addition, the Church should foster interfaith and interethnic dialogue. Promoting understanding and cooperation among different religious and ethnic groups can contribute to social cohesion and political stability. These dialogues can help address the root causes of political tensions and promote a culture of peace and reconciliation.

Also, the Church should engage in partnerships with civil society organisations. Collaborating with non-governmental organisations (NGOs), community groups, and other faith-based organisations can amplify the Church's advocacy efforts and help reach a broader audience. These partnerships can facilitate the pooling of resources, sharing of expertise, and coordination of actions to address social and political issues more effectively. For example, partnerships with organisations focused on anti-corruption, human rights, and electoral integrity can enhance the Church's impact in these areas.

Political Education

Political education is another crucial aspect of the political engagement for Catholic priests. Educating the congregation about their civic responsibilities, the political process, and the importance of voting is essential for fostering informed and active participation in democratic governance. The Catholic Bishops' Conference of Nigeria (CBCN) has consistently emphasised the role of the Church in political education, urging Priests to encourage critical thinking and informed political participation (Catholic Bishops' Conference of Nigeria, 2019).

Through sermons, workshops, and educational programs, Priests help their congregations understand the significance of their political rights and responsibilities. They discuss the importance of voting, the workings of the political system, and the impact of policies on everyday life. This educational effort is grounded in the Church's commitment to human dignity and the common good, as articulated in various encyclicals and official documents.

A biblical reference that underscores the importance of political engagement is found in Romans 13:1, where Paul writes, *"Let everyone be subject to the governing authorities, for there is no authority except that which God has established."* This passage highlights the role of Christians in participating in and respecting the political order while also holding it accountable to God's standards of justice and righteousness.

In addition to biblical references, the Church's social teachings provide a strong foundation for political education. *Lumen Gentium* emphasises the Church's role in guiding the faithful in all aspects of life, including political engagement. It calls for a holistic approach to evangelization that addresses both spiritual and temporal needs (Lumen Gentium, 1964). This comprehensive perspective encourages Priests to integrate political education into their pastoral duties, helping their congregations navigate the complexities of the political landscape.

Case Study: The Catholic Church's Role in Nigeria's 2015 General Elections

The 2015 general elections in Nigeria provide a pertinent example of the Catholic Church's active engagement in the political process. Leading up to the elections, the Catholic Bishops' Conference of Nigeria (CBCN) issued a pastoral letter emphasising the importance of free, fair, and credible elections. They called on all Nigerians to exercise their voting rights responsibly and urged political candidates to prioritise the common good over personal ambition.

On Election Day, the Church deployed thousands of observers across the country to monitor the electoral process. The JDPC played a crucial role in training and coordinating these observers, ensuring that they were well-prepared to identify and report any irregularities. The Church's involvement helped to promote transparency and accountability, contributing to the relatively peaceful conduct of the elections.

Furthermore, the Church's leaders engaged in post-election reconciliation efforts. Recognising the potential for post-election violence, the CBCN and other Catholic organisations called for calm and urged political leaders and their supporters to respect the outcome of the elections. This proactive stance helped to mitigate tensions and foster a spirit of reconciliation in the aftermath of the elections.

Through sustained and strategic engagement, the Catholic Church in Nigeria can continue to be a beacon of hope and a catalyst for positive change, ensuring that faith and politics intersect in ways that promote the well-being of all Nigerians. The road towards this goal requires ongoing reflection, dialogue, and action, grounded in the timeless values of the Gospel and the rich tradition of Catholic social teaching.

The Impact of Political Instability on the Christian Faith

Political instability can manifest in various forms, including conflicts, corruption, and bad governance, among many others. These factors can create an environment of uncertainty and fear, which can hinder religious practices. For instance, in regions plagued by conflict, churches may face difficulties in holding regular services, conducting outreach programs, and providing spiritual and social support to their communities. The Catholic Church, with her extensive network and commitment to social justice, often steps in to fill the gaps left by failing political systems, offering solace and aid to those affected.

One real-life example of this can be seen in the Middle Belt region of Nigeria, where inter-communal violence has disrupted the lives of many. In this context, the Catholic Church has played a significant role in providing not only spiritual guidance but also material support. Through initiatives such as peace-building workshops and humanitarian aid, the Church has helped to restore a sense of normalcy and hope to communities torn apart by violence. This aligns with the Church's teachings on social justice and the call to be peacemakers, as emphasised in the Beatitudes, *"Blessed are the peacemakers, for they will be called children of God"* (Matthew 5:9, NIV).

One major impact of political instability is the strain it places on religious leaders. Priests and other clergy members often find themselves on the frontlines, advocating for peace and justice while also tending to the spiritual needs of their congregations. The pressure can be enormous, but it is also an opportunity for the Church to demonstrate her commitment to the common good. The courage and commitment of these faith leaders is a testament to their faith and belief in the power of the Gospel to transform lives and communities. Father Michael, a Priest from a conflict zone, noted, "Despite the risks, I have to continue to serve the community by celebrating Mass and providing support to those in need." His story reminds us of the resilience of faith and the Church's mission to help the marginalised and oppressed, and this echoes the words of Pope Francis in *Evangelii Gaudium,* "The Church which 'goes forth' is a community of missionary disciples who take the first step, who are involved and supportive, who bear fruit and rejoice" (Evangelii Gaudium, 24).

Political instability also has a great impact on the youth, who are often the most vulnerable in such situations. The Catholic Church in Nigeria has made significant efforts to engage with young people, offering them a sense of purpose and hope through faith-based programs and activities. By fostering a sense of community and belonging, the Church helps to counteract the negative effects of political instability on the younger generation. This is important, as the youth are the future of the Church and the nation. In areas affected by political unrest, the role of churches in education is becoming more important. Catholic schools and institutions often serve as a haven for children, providing moral and spiritual training in addition to academic education. This school is a place where young people can learn about their faith and develop a sense of social responsibility. The Church's teaching on human dignity and the common good, as expressed in documents such as *Lumen Gentium* and *Nostra Aetate*, provides a strong foundation for this holistic approach to education (Second Vatican Council, Lumen Gentium, 1964); Second Vatican Council, Nostra Aetate, 1965).

Political instability also affects the ability of the Church to fulfil her social mission. In many places where churches are the main providers of social services such as health care, education, and relief for the poor, political instability disrupts the provision of these services, and it is often the most vulnerable members of society who suffer the most.

However, the Church's efforts to maintain these services during turbulent times demonstrate her commitment to the Gospel message of love and service and her role as a beacon of hope and a source of stability in turbulent times. An example of this can be seen in the Church's response to the Boko Haram insurgency in northeastern Nigeria. Despite these risks, churches continue to provide essential services to those affected.

Political instability may lead to increased persecution of Christians and other religious minorities. In such situations, churches are often targets of violence and oppression. However, it also provides an opportunity for the Church to demonstrate the strength of her faith and her commitment to supporting the oppressed. The testimonies of those who have suffered for their faith are powerful reminders of the cost of discipleship and the call to bear witness to the Gospel, even in the face of persecution. One such testimony comes from a community in northern Nigeria that has suffered severe persecution. Despite threats and attacks, members of this community continued to gather to worship and support one another. Their faith and perseverance despite such adversity is a testament to the power of the Gospel and the power of the Christian community.

The Church's response to political instability involves more than providing immediate aid and support. This includes efforts to find long-term solutions that address the root causes of instability. This includes advocating for good governance, promoting social justice, and working toward reconciliation and peace. The Church's teaching on human dignity and the common good provides a solid foundation for this activity (Pope Paul VI, People's Development, 1967).

In their outreach efforts, churches often work in collaboration with other religious and civil society organisations. This collaboration helps in addressing the challenges posed by political instability. By working together, these organisations can amplify their voices and increase their impact. The Church's commitment to dialogue and collaboration is a reflection of her belief in the importance of building bridges and working towards the common good.

Addressing Social Injustices Through Authentic Witnessing

Addressing social injustices through Christian witnessing and ministry is a fundamental aspect of the Church's mission, especially in Nigeria. The Church has been a vocal voice for all, promoting social justice and good governance, enhancing human dignity, and allowing for a just and egalitarian society.

One of the primary ways the Catholic Church in Nigeria addresses social injustices is through education. The Church runs numerous schools and educational programs aimed at providing quality education to underprivileged children. This plan is based on the belief that education is a powerful tool for social change, as Pope Francis emphasised: "Education is an act of hope" (Laudato Si', 202). And so, education is a cornerstone of the Church's efforts to empower communities and break the cycle of poverty. For example, the Catholic Archdiocese of Lagos (as in countless dioceses around the world and Nigerian in particular) opened several schools in low-income areas and provided scholarships to students who could not afford to pay tuition. These schools provide not only academic education but also instil moral values and social responsibility in students. Likewise, the Diocese of Sokoto has implemented an initiative called 'Hope Schools' targeting children from nomadic communities who have traditionally had no access to formal education and offering portable classrooms and flexible schedules for them to receive an education.

Health care is another crucial aspect of life in which the Church has made a significant contribution. Catholic hospitals and clinics across Nigeria provide essential medical services, often in regions where healthcare facilities are scarce or non-existent. The St. Gerard Catholic Hospital in Kaduna is a notable example, offering affordable and sometimes free medical care to those in need. This hospital has become a beacon of hope for many, demonstrating the Church's commitment to alleviating suffering and promoting health and well-being. According to the Pontifical Council for Pastoral Assistance to Health Care Workers, "The

Church is called to manifest the love of God in the field of health care" (Christifideles Laici, 54).

The Church also engages in advocacy and direct action to address social injustices. The Justice, Development, and Peace Commission (JDPC) of the Catholic Church in Nigeria is actively involved in various social justice issues, including human rights, economic inequality, and environmental sustainability. JDPC's programs are designed to empower communities, promote justice, and foster sustainable development. For instance, the JDPC in the Diocese of Ijebu-Ode has implemented numerous projects aimed at improving agricultural practices, thus enhancing food security and reducing poverty. These initiatives align with the Church's teaching on the preferential option for the poor, as stated in the *Compendium of the Social Doctrine of the Church*, "Love for the poor is incompatible with immoderate love of riches or their selfish use" (CSDC, 329).

The Church's efforts to address social injustices are also evident in her response to crises. During the uprising in northeastern Nigeria, the Catholic Church played an important role in helping internally displaced people (IDPs). Catholic Relief Services (CRS) worked with local dioceses to provide food, shelter and psychological support to thousands of internally displaced people. These interventions not only alleviated immediate suffering but also helped restore the lives of those affected by the conflict following the teachings of Christ, *"For I was hungry, and you gave me food; I was thirsty, and you gave me drink; I was a stranger, and you took me in"* (Matthew 25:35).

The Church's role in conflict resolution and peace-building is also important. In regions suffering from ethnic and religious violence, the Church has played an important role in promoting dialogue and reconciliation. The Archdiocese of Jos, for example, has established peace-building initiatives that bring together Christians and Muslims to promote mutual understanding and cooperation. These efforts are grounded in the Church's teaching on the dignity of the human person and the call to be peacemakers, as stated in the encyclical *Pacem in Terris* by Pope John XXIII: "Peace on earth, which man throughout the ages has so longed for and sought after, can never be established, never guaranteed, except by the diligent observance of the divinely established order" (Pacem in Terris, 1).

Personal stories from Priests and laypeople involved in these initiatives add a human dimension to the Church's work. Father Patrick, a parish Priest in the Diocese of Makurdi, in sharing his experience of working with JDPC to provide legal aid to victims of human trafficking, recounts a case where a young girl, trafficked and exploited, was rescued and reintegrated into society through the combined efforts of the Church and local authorities. This story highlights the tangible impact of the Church's commitment to justice and human dignity. Sister Mary, a nun working at her rural health clinic, describes the challenges and benefits of providing health care in remote areas. She spoke of a mother walking miles to bring her sick child to the hospital and the joy of seeing her child restored to health.

The Church's advocacy for social justice extends to addressing systemic issues. For instance, the Catholic Bishops' Conference of Nigeria (CBCN) has been vocal in calling for good governance and accountability. In their pastoral letters, the bishops consistently urge political leaders to uphold justice, combat corruption, and promote the common good. This prophetic voice is crucial in a context where political instability and corruption often exacerbate social injustices. As stated in *Gaudium et Spes*, "The Church, by reason of her role and competence, is not identified in any way with the political community nor bound to any political system. She is, at once, a sign and a safeguard of the transcendental dimension of the human person" (Gaudium et Spes, 76).

The Church's commitment to social justice is also reflected in her environmental initiatives. In response to Pope Francis's encyclical *Laudato Si'*, many dioceses in Nigeria have launched programs to promote environmental sustainability. These include tree-planting campaigns, clean-up drives, and educational programs on environmental stewardship. The Diocese of Enugu, for instance, has been actively involved in reforestation projects aimed at combating deforestation and preserving the ecosystem. These efforts demonstrate the Church's holistic approach to social justice, recognising that caring for the environment is integral to caring for humanity. As Pope Francis writes, "We need to strengthen the conviction that we are one single human family" (Laudato Si', 52).

The Church also plays a crucial role in promoting economic justice. Through microfinance programs and cooperatives, the Church helps individuals and families improve their economic standing. The Catholic Caritas Foundation of Nigeria (CCFN) has implemented microfinance initiatives that provide small loans to entrepreneurs, particularly women, to start or expand their businesses. This support not only boosts local economies but also empowers individuals to become self-reliant and contribute to their communities. The success of these programs is evident in the stories of beneficiaries who have been able to lift themselves out of poverty and provide for their families.

Furthermore, the Church's involvement in addressing social injustices extends to the legal arena. The Catholic Lawyers Association in Nigeria offers pro bono legal services to those who cannot afford representation, particularly in cases involving human rights abuse. This initiative ensures that justice is accessible to all, regardless of their socio-economic status. By standing up for the marginalised and oppressed, the Church embodies the biblical call to *"defend the rights of the poor and needy"* (Proverbs 31:9).

The impact of the Church's work in addressing social injustices is also evident in her partnerships with other organisations and government bodies. By collaborating with NGOs, international agencies, and local governments, the Church amplifies her efforts and reaches a broader audience. These partnerships are crucial in addressing complex social issues that require a multifaceted approach. For instance, the Church's collaboration with UNICEF on child protection programs has led to significant improvements in the safety and well-being of children in conflict-affected areas.

In addition to these initiatives, the Church also focuses on empowering the youth. Recognising the potential of young people to drive social change, the Church invests in youth development programs that provide education, vocational training, and leadership development. The Young Christian Workers (YCW) movement in Nigeria, for example, equips young people with the skills and knowledge needed to advocate for social justice and contribute to the development of their communities. This focus on youth empowerment is in line with the Church's teaching that young people are "the hope of the future" (Christus Vivit, 64).

The Church's commitment to addressing social injustices is also reflected in her liturgical and sacramental life. The celebration of the sacraments, particularly the Eucharist, is a powerful expression of the Church's solidarity with the poor and marginalised. In his encyclical *Ecclesia de Eucharistia,* Pope John Paul II emphasised, "The Eucharist commits us to the poor and compels us to work for justice" (Ecclesia de Eucharistia, 20). By integrating social justice into her liturgical life, the Church constantly reminds her faithful of their call to be agents of change in society.

The Church's teaching on social justice is deeply rooted in her theological foundations. The principles of Catholic Social Teaching, including the dignity of the human person, the common good, subsidiarity, and solidarity, provide a framework for the Church's efforts to address social injustices. These principles are not just theoretical concepts but are lived out through the Church's ministry and actions. As stated in the *Compendium of the Social Doctrine of the Church*, "The Church's social teaching is a privileged instrument of dialogue between the Gospel and the Church.

The Church's Role in Peace-Building

In a world full of conflict and division, the Catholic Church plays a vital role in promoting peace and reconciliation, mediation and conflict transformation. In the Sermon on the Mount, Jesus taught that peacemaking is a characteristic of Christian discipleship. He says, "*Blessed are the peacemakers, for they will be called children of God*" (Matthew 5:9). This Beatitude is not just a blessing but a call to action, and it reminds us that peace is not just a goal, but a fundamental aspect of our Christian identity. We are called to be peacemakers, to strive for unity and mutual understanding, and to work to build a more harmonious world. The Cardinal Onaiyekan Foundation for Peace is a perfect reflection of a true response to the mission of Christianity and the universal call for peace by building leaders' capacity across the board and beyond the Church and with other religions across Africa.

The Church's role in peace-building is rooted in the above biblical understanding and is implemented through a variety of activities and programs aimed at promoting peace and reconciliation. One of such is the promotion of a culture of respect and love through her teaching on human dignity. As stated in *Gaudium et Spes*, "Every human being is endowed with dignity and therefore must be treated with respect and love" (Gaudium et Spes, 1965). This teaching reminds us that all people have intrinsic value and should be treated with compassion and understanding.

The Church also promotes peace by advocating for justice. As stated in the encyclical *Pacem in Terris*, "Peace is the fruit of justice and mercy" (Pacem in Terris, 1963). This teaching reminds us that peace is not only the absence of conflict but also the presence of justice and mercy. It is rooted in biblical understanding, as seen in Isaiah 58:6-7, where it is written, "*Is not this the fast that I choose: to loose the bonds of injustice, to undo the thongs of the yoke, to let the oppressed go free, and to break every yoke? Is it not to share your bread with the hungry and bring the homeless poor into your house?*" We are reminded that justice is not just a moral obligation but a fundamental aspect of our faith. The Church's advocacy for justice is also lived out through her teaching of the common good. As stated in the document *Gaudium et Spes*, "The common good is the sum of those conditions of social life which allow social groups and their individual members relatively thorough and ready access to their own fulfilment" (Gaudium et Spes, 1965). This teaching reminds us that justice is not just an individual virtue but a social one. The Church's defence of justice is a very important aspect of promoting peace and non-violence. By advocating for justice and working to address the root causes of conflict, the Church helps build a peaceful and harmonious world. We Catholics are called to join this advocacy.

The sacraments and liturgy of the Church are powerful tools for peace-building. The Eucharist, in particular, is a powerful symbol of unity and reconciliation, reminding us that we are all one in Christ. The *Lumen Gentium* documentation says, "The Eucharist is the source and summit of Christian life" (Lumen

Gentium, 1964). Additionally, *Sacrosanctum Concilium* states, "The liturgy is the summit toward which the activity of the Church is directed; at the same time, it is the font from which all her power flows" (Sacrosanctum Concilium, 1963). The liturgy is not just a ritual but a source of strength and inspiration for our lives. Participating in the Liturgy and Eucharist reminds us of our unity with Christ and with one another, and we are inspired to work to build a more peaceful and harmonious world.

Additionally, the Church's sacraments and liturgy are a source of comfort and strength in times of conflict and violence. *Gaudium et Spes* document states, "The Church has the duty to proclaim the Kingdom of God and his justice and to condemn the injustice and cruelty suffered by the world" (Gaudium et Spes, 1965). Faith is not only a source of comfort but also a source of strength and courage. As Catholics, we are called to embrace this teaching and work towards building a more just and peaceful society.

The Church's teachings on forgiveness and mercy are powerful tools for peacemaking. As Jesus taught us, *"Forgive us our debts, as we forgive our debtors"* (Matthew 6:12). This teaching reminds us that forgiveness is a choice, not just a feeling. By choosing to forgive, we can break the cycle of violence and revenge and become peaceful.

The Catholic Church's teaching on the dignity of the human person is another fundamental aspect of promoting peace and non-violence. *Gaudium et Spes.* state, "Every human person is endowed with dignity, and therefore should be treated with respect and love" (Gaudium et Spes., 1965). This teaching is rooted in Genesis 1:26-27, *"Then God said, 'Let us make man in our image, after our likeness... So God created man in his own image, in the image of God he created him; male and female he created them."* This passage reminds us that every human being is created in the image and likeness of God and, therefore, has inherent value and worth. By recognising the inherent value and worth of every person, we are reminded that we are all children of God and, therefore, brothers and sisters to one another. The encyclical *Pacem in Terris* states, "All people are equal in inherent dignity. Therefore, all forms of discrimination on the grounds of race, colour, gender, social status or religion are contrary to the heart of Christ" (Pacem in Teris, 1963).

The Church's teaching on human dignity is also put into practice by protecting the poor and marginalised. As stated in the document *Evangelii Gaudium,* "The Church is especially concerned about the poor, and this is a fundamental part of her mission" (Evangelii Gaudium, 2013). We are reminded that poor and marginalised people are not mere statistics or numbers but people with inherent dignity and worth, and by defending their rights and dignity, the Church helps build a more just and peaceful society. The Church's teaching on human dignity is also a powerful tool for promoting forgiveness and reconciliation. As noted in *Dives in Misericordia*, "Forgiveness is a fundamental aspect of the Church's teaching on mercy" (Dives in Misericordia, 1980). We are taught that forgiveness is a choice, not just a feeling. By choosing forgiveness, we can break the cycle of violence and revenge and work to build a peaceful and harmonious world.

In Nigeria, the Church's role in peace-building is particularly important. Nigeria has a diverse population and complex social and political problems that require constant promotion of peace and reconciliation, and the Church continues to do exceptional work there. As followers of Christ, the Church calls us to support and encourage this work.

Ethical Considerations and Challenges to the Christian

The Christian faith provides a robust framework for political participation, emphasising the importance of justice, peace, and the common good driven by the core Gospel values of love and service as the motivating drive for the intentions for participation in politics. In Nigeria, Christians are called and encouraged to engage actively in political life, addressing the nation's challenges with integrity, a commitment to ethical principles, and consciousness of the Gospel values. By doing so, they contribute to building a just and humane society rooted in the values of the Gospel.

However, political participation in Nigeria is fraught with challenges, including corruption, electoral fraud, and violence. Christians must navigate these challenges with a strong ethical compass guided by their faith. To this effect, certain salient ethical considerations must be kept in mind:

Integrity and Accountability: Christian politicians and public servants are called to demonstrate integrity and accountability in their actions by being transparent in their dealings, avoiding corrupt practices, and being accountable to the people they serve.

Promoting the Common Good: The primary aim of political engagement should be promoting the common good. Christians and Catholics, in particular, are encouraged to support policies and initiatives that benefit all members of society, especially the poor and marginalised.

Respect for Human Dignity: All political actions and decisions should respect and uphold the dignity of every human person. This principle is central to Catholic social teaching and informs the Church's stance on various social and political issues.

While striving for more positive political participation, challenges are bound to happen. Nigeria's political landscape presents specific challenges that affect Christian participation, such as:

Religious Persecution and Discrimination: In certain regions, Christians face persecution and discrimination, which can hinder their ability to participate fully in political life. Addressing these issues requires a concerted effort to promote religious freedom and tolerance.

Ethno-Religious Conflicts: The interplay between ethnic and religious identities can lead to conflicts that complicate political participation. Christians must work towards fostering unity and understanding among diverse groups.

Socio-Economic Inequalities: Widespread poverty and inequality can marginalise certain populations, making it difficult for them to engage in political processes. The Church's social justice initiatives aim to address these root causes and empower all citizens to participate in governance.

The Catholic Church encourages the faithful to participate in political life as a means of promoting the common good and upholding justice and human dignity. The Second Vatican Council's document, *Gaudium et Spes*, underscores the importance of political engagement, stating. "The Church praises and esteems the work of those who, for the good of humankind, devote themselves to the service of the state and take on the burdens of this office" (Vatican II, 1965). Pope John Paul II, in his encyclical *Christifideles Laici*, further emphasised the role of lay Christians in political life, highlighting their duty to imbue temporal realities with the values of the Gospel (John Paul II, 1988). This theological foundation urges Christians to be active participants in shaping a just and humane society.

CHAPTER IV

The Catholic Priest and Advocacy for Social Justice

Pope John Paul II, in his encyclical *Sollicitudo Rei Socialis*, highlighted the importance of solidarity and the preferential option for the poor, urging Christians to work towards a society where the dignity of every person is respected and protected (John Paul II, 1987). These teachings provide a robust framework for Catholic Priests in Nigeria to engage in social justice advocacy. The Catholic Church's commitment to social justice is deeply rooted in her theological teachings.

The Second Vatican Council's document, *Gaudium et Spes*, emphasises the Church's duty to be deeply involved in the socio-economic realities of the world, stating, "The joys and the hopes, the griefs and the anxieties of the men of this age, especially those who are poor or in any way afflicted, these are the joys and hopes, the griefs and anxieties of the followers of Christ" (Vatican II, 1965).

The role of the Catholic Priest extends beyond spiritual guidance and pastoral care; it encompasses a profound commitment to advocating for social justice. In Nigeria, a country grappling with issues of corruption, inequality, and violence, Catholic Priests are often at the forefront of efforts to promote human dignity, justice, and peace. Here, we take a look at how Catholic Priests in Nigeria engage in social justice advocacy, drawing on Church teachings and their own experiences. Promoting justice is an integral part of the Priests' faith and mission. Faith and action go hand in hand, and commitment to peace and justice is essential to the success of living out the Christian faith. Scripture says, "*Brothers, how good is it for a man to profess his faith but have nothing to show for it?*" (James 2:14).

Priests often act as prophetic voices, speaking out against injustices such as corruption, human rights abuses, and socio-economic inequalities. This has often been amplified by the Catholic Bishops' Conference of Nigeria (CBCN) and its frequent issuing of pastoral letters and statements addressing these issues and calling for ethical governance and respect for human dignity. Priests also engage with local communities as mobilizers and community organisers. This involves mobilising resources, facilitating discussions, and leading initiatives that aim to improve the living conditions of the poor and marginalised. Through community organising, Priests help to empower individuals and communities to take collective action for social change.

Furthermore, given that the education of the whole human person is holistic and should be wholesome, education is a vital tool for social justice, and so Catholic Priests often engage in educating their congregations about their rights and responsibilities. They advocate for policies that promote social justice and work to raise awareness about issues affecting their communities. By doing so, they help to build an informed and active citizenry.

Finally, in regions affected by conflict and violence, Priests often act as mediators and peace-builders. They facilitate dialogue between conflicting parties, promote reconciliation, and work towards restoring peace and harmony. This role is particularly important in Nigeria, where ethnic and religious tensions frequently lead to violence.

The Catholic Church and Her Social Teachings

The social teachings of the Catholic Church constitute a general teaching on the belief in the dignity of every human being and the importance of participation in the life of society. This teaching reflects the relationship of Catholics to society by emphasising the principles of harmony, solidarity, and the interests of the poor.

Catholic social teaching is built on a set of core principles that reflect the Church's commitment to justice, peace, and the dignity of every human being. These principles are articulated in various Church documents and encyclicals and form the foundation for the Church's social doctrine. The social teachings of the Catholic Church provide a rich and comprehensive framework for addressing contemporary social issues. The principles that are integral to the Church's social teachings and position are:

1. Human Dignity: The belief that every person is created in the image and likeness of God and therefore possesses inherent dignity and worth. This principle is the cornerstone of all Catholic social teaching.

2. The Common Good: The notion that society should be organised so that all people can flourish and achieve their full potential. This involves promoting social conditions that allow for the well-being of all members of society.

3. Solidarity: The recognition of our interconnectedness and the responsibility to care for one another, especially the poor and marginalised. Solidarity calls for a commitment to the common good and active engagement in the promotion of social justice.

4. Subsidiarity: The principle that social and political issues should be addressed at the most local level possible, empowering individuals and communities to take action on their own behalf.

5. Preferential Option for the Poor: The imperative to prioritise the needs of the poor and vulnerable in all social, economic, and political decisions.

6. Care for Creation: The call to steward and protect the environment is part of our responsibility to God and future generations.

Human Dignity

The concept of human dignity is fundamental to the social teaching of the Catholic Church. According to *Gaudium et Spes*, "Human dignity derives from humanity created in the image and likeness of God" (GS, 12). This principle clearly states that every human being has inherent values that must be respected and protected. Belief in human dignity is not only a theological affirmation but also a call to action. It requires all aspects of society, from laws to institutions, from business to culture, to recognise and foster this dignity.

Human dignity also requires the recognition of human rights. *Pacem in Terris* says, "Every human being is endowed with wisdom and freedom, and therefore with rights and responsibilities" (PT, 9). These rights include the rights to life, food, clothing, shelter, education, and employment. They also include civil and political rights such as freedom of expression, religion, and assembly. The

Church's emphasis on human dignity is central to her worldwide struggle for justice and human rights.

Delegation of Authority

Delegation of authority is another important issue of Catholic discipline. This principle emphasises the importance of supporting local communities and small organisations in managing their own affairs and solving problems that directly affect them.

Delegation encourages a bottom-up approach to management and decision-making, enabling senior officials to support rather than hinder local efforts. It respects the freedom and initiative of individuals and small communities and encourages awareness of responsibility and cooperation. This principle is particularly important in solving social problems because it encourages social solutions and community participation while also ensuring that higher authorities provide the necessary support and resources.

Solidarity

Solidarity is a way of demonstrating the unity of the people and the importance of working together for the common good. It is the basis for understanding that, despite our differences, we are all part of the human family. According to *Sollicitudo Rei Socialis*, "Solidarity is a firm determination and action to work for the common good, that is, for the benefit of each and every one, because each of us is truly responsible for everyone" (SRS, 38).

Solidarity should be directed towards the welfare of others, especially the poor and needy. It requires action to address injustice and inequality and recognition that our own well-being is intertwined with the well-being of others. This principle is often explained by the concept of 'negative interests', which refers to the importance of the needs and rights of the poor in the decision-making and distribution of the capital layer.

The Importance of the Poor

The importance of the poor is also at the foundation of Catholic social teaching. It is especially marked for the poor and needy in society. This principle is based on the biblical tradition of God's concern for the poor and oppressed, as illustrated in passages such as Proverbs 31:8–9: *"Speak for those who cannot speak for themselves and for all who have need of justice."*

The best option for the poor is not just charity but also addressing the root causes of poverty and injustice. It is necessary to change the system to ensure that the poor have access to resources and opportunities and have a say in the decisions that affect their lives. Recalling *Centesimus Annus*, "The needs of the poor come before the needs of the rich; the rights of workers come before profits" (CA, 35).

Peace and Justice

The pursuit of peace and justice is part of the discipline of the Church. Peace is not just the absence of war but also the presence of justice and harmony in society. According to *Pacem in Terris*, "The world peace that men desire and find everywhere in the world cannot be created and guaranteed except by their efforts to obey God's command" (PT, 1). This divine order includes respecting human rights, promoting goodness, and ensuring justice for all.

In the Catholic tradition, justice is understood as giving everyone their due. It includes communicative justice (fair exchange between people) and fairness (justice and social processes). Social justice requires addressing inequality and ensuring that everyone has access to the resources and opportunities they need to live with dignity. Referring to the connection between the social and the peaceful, Pope Paul VI emphasised in his encyclical letter, "Construction is the new name of peace" (PP, 76).

Guardianship of Creation

In recent years, the Catholic Church has increased the importance of caring for the environment as part of her social teaching. Pope Francis's encyclical on the environment, *Laudato Si*, calls for a new dialogue on the future of our world (LS, 14). The circular emphasises the interdependence of all creation and the need for sustainable development that respects human dignity and the environment.

The care of creation is care for the earth and its resources, as we see that these are God's gifts designed to help everyone. It requires accountability and sustainability in the use of resources and solving problems such as pollution, climate change and environmental degradation. This principle has its roots in the Bible in Genesis 2:15; here, humans are called to '*reign and rule*' the earth, that is, to cultivate and protect it.

Family and Society

The Catholic Church teaches that the family is the foundation of society and the centre from which people learn to fulfil their roles in society. According to *Familiaris Consortio*, "The family is the first school and main institution of social life: as a community of love, it finds within itself the authority that guides and develops it" (FC, 37). The health and stability of the family directly affect the health of the entire society.

Catholic social teaching also emphasises living in a community outside the family. Humans are social animals designed to live in relationships with others. According to *Caritas in Veritate,* "To love someone means to want the good of that person and to do good for him" (CV, 7). The relationship between humans requires participation in the life of society and a commitment to relationships based on mutual respect, care and cooperation.

The Role of the Church

The Catholic Church sees herself as a community of Christians. Her purpose is not only to preach the Gospel but also to promote justice, peace and harmony among people. According to *Lumen Gentium*, "The Church, both visible and spiritual, is as a reality the nation of God's people and the body of Christ" (LG, 8). The two natures of the Church include a commitment to both spiritual and social aspects of human life. The role of the Church in teaching relationships is to ensure morality and promote justice and peace. The mission of the Church is to bear witness, through her teachings and actions, to the importance and power of the Gospel for positive change in the world.

The principles of Catholic discipline are not only theoretical but also practical recommendations for solving today's problems. They provide an ethical framework for evaluating policies, practices, and institutions to promote human dignity, fairness, and justice. In today's world, these principles can be applied in many areas, such as economic justice, political cooperation, environmental security, and sharing global pressure.

Social Justice

Social Justice is concerned with ensuring that policies that promote the well-being of all, especially the poor and marginalised, are instituted. This includes fair wages, fair distribution, and meaningful work. According to *Laborem Exercens*, "Work is good for man, a good thing for humanity, for through work man not only changes nature to suit his needs but also succeeds as men succeed" (LE, 9). The Church teaches that work is not just a product but an essential part of human dignity. Therefore, business models must respect the dignity of employees by ensuring fair wages and job security.

Principles of economic justice require accountability for wealth and resources. Wealth should not be used for personal gain but should be used for the benefit of the people. As stated in *Rerum Novarum,* "Let workers and employers be able to agree on wages, and especially to agree freely; this should be done even if wages are not sufficient to support health and financial well-being" (NWS, 45). This reflects the Church's view that business should serve people's needs and promote goodness.

Participation in politics also serves as a means of promoting justice and relationships. According to *Gaudium et Spes*, "Every citizen must remember his right and duty to use his free vote to promote good" (GS, 75). Political participation is seen as an expression of solidarity and a way to influence the norms and policies that affect people's lives. Political rights should be exercised morally and with consent. *Dignitatis Humanae* emphasises the importance of freedom of religion and the right of people to participate in public life according to their conscience (DH, 2). This includes voting, participating in public discussions, and holding board meetings.

Environmental Sustainability

Environmental sustainability is an increasing topic of interest in Catholic teaching and is particularly important in *Laudato Si*. The encyclical calls for a significant ecology that recognises the interaction of all creation and solves social and environmental problems. According to *Laudato Si*, "The cry of the world and the cry of the poor are one and the same" (LS, 49). These words reflect the Church's understanding that environmental degradation negatively affects the poor and vulnerable.

Environmental management involves careful attention to the creation and use of resources. It calls for sustainable practices to protect the planet for future generations. *Laudato Si'* demonstrates the need for an ecological shift, that is, a change in the way we view our relationship with nature. This includes reducing waste, saving resources, and promoting renewable energy. By advocating environmental sustainability, the Church integrates her work with the broader goal of protecting God's creation and making the world livable for all.

Global Solidarity

In this increasingly interconnected world, the principle of international solidarity is more important than ever. The Church teaches that we are part of a global community that has a responsibility to those beyond our borders. According to *Sollicitudo Rei Socialis*, "Solidarity helps us see the other, whether a person, a society or a nation, as more than a tool, with the ability to work and the energy of physical presence that can be used at a low cost, then thrown aside when they are no longer useful, but our neighbour, our helper, our partner in the celebration of life to which God invites everyone equally" (SRS, 39).

Global solidarity is the solution to worldwide problems of poverty, inequality, and injustice. It requires the cooperation of countries and the promotion of human rights and development for all. The Church advocates for fair trade, debt relief for developing countries, and international aid that supports communities. By fostering a sense of universal solidarity, Catholics can help build a world where the dignity and rights of all people are respected.

In totality, the social teachings of the Catholic Church provide a rich basis for solving today's social problems. Based on the principles of human dignity, kindness, cooperation, unity and governance, these teachings call for a just society where everyone's total well-being is important. Drawing on scriptural principles and the documents of the Church, the Church provides ethics and solutions to create a world that reflects the importance of justice, peace and human dignity.

Priests as Social Crusaders for Justice

Catholic priests, often seen as spiritual teachers and religious leaders, play the role of social agents. These qualities are not limited to principles; they are on the front lines of social justice, fighting on behalf of marginalised groups and fighting injustice. This changing role, deeply rooted in Christ and the teaching of the Catholic Church, challenges Priests to become agents of change in their communities.

Priests as Voices for the Voiceless

In Nigeria, where economic inequality and social injustice are rife, Priests often defend those who cannot speak for themselves. They address issues such as poverty, corruption, and human rights violations. For example, in rural communities, pastors may be leaders in providing clean water, education, and health care, while in cities, they may create resistance to violence or dishonesty.

A good example of this is Fr. Patrick Ngoyi, in the Niger Delta, working tirelessly to protect the environment from oil spills. His initiative brought attention to the problems of poor communities and put pressure on the government and oil companies to solve the problems. The likes of names and faces of John Cardinal Onaiyekan, Archbishop Ignatius Kaiama of Abuja, Bishop Godfrey Onah of Nsukka in the South East, Bishop Matthew Hassan Kukah in faraway Sokoto, Rev. Fr. George Ehusani as well as many others in like manner have remained prophetic voices in our generation speaking truth to power at all times.

Impact of Priest's Initiative

The leadership of the Catholic Priest brought about real change in Nigerian society. Their efforts led to policy changes, awareness of social problems, and improved conditions for disadvantaged groups. For example, advocacy against human trafficking by Priests and religious organisations has resulted in better laws and protection of victims.

Also, the Church's involvement in education and health care has had a lasting impact. Catholic schools and hospitals, often run by Priests, provide important services to communities that might otherwise be underserved. These organisations not only address current needs but also contribute to the long-term development of society.

Catholic Priests in Nigeria are not only spiritual leaders but also active in social change work. Their commitment to justice, based on the teachings of the Bible and the teachings of the Church, leads them to solve today's social problems. Despite the many challenges they face, their initiatives and actions continue to make a huge impact, providing hope and support to society's most vulnerable members.

Challenges and Opportunities

In Nigeria's changing environment, Catholic Priests play an important role in advocating for justice and peace. However, their roles are not without challenges and opportunities. Understanding these changes is crucial to understanding the enormous impact of evidence on society.

One of the biggest challenges facing Catholic Priests in Nigeria is mutual distrust and conflict. The country's history of insurgency, civil strife, and corruption creates an environment where social justice advocacy can be dangerous. Pastors often find themselves in a dangerous situation when they speak out against injustices created by those in power. As seen in the scriptures, the Priest's prophetic role, like the experience of the prophets in the Old Testament, often leads to confrontation with the law. Jeremiah 1:19 says, "*They will fight you, but they will not prevail against you; for I am with you, says the LORD, and I will save you.*"

Material poverty is another challenge. Many parts of Nigeria are mired in poverty, resulting in inequality and injustice. A Priest working in a poor area and witnessing the struggle of his parishioners may have limited resources to help alleviate the social distress of those in need. However, as stated in *Gaudium et Spes*, the Church's teaching demonstrates the need to address the root causes of suffering: "These are the joy and hope, the sorrow and anxiety of this age, especially those who are poor or depressed, even though they suffer. It is the joy and hope of the Christian, his sadness and anxiety" (Gaudium et Spes, 1).

Culture and religion are also problematic. Nigeria is a country full of ethnic and religious diversity, which can sometimes lead to violence and conflict. Priests must walk this difficult path while promoting unity and peace. The Church's commitment to ecumenism and dialogue is essential in this context, as stated in *Nostra Aetate*: "The Church condemns all forms of discrimination or harassment against people because of their difference in race and colour.

Many Priests begin their studies with a good religious foundation but may not have the necessary skills to deal with difficult situations. This gap can be addressed through the continued formation and support of the Church to ensure that Priests can serve the community.

Other serious challenges include resistance from within their own institutions and communities, political and economic pressures to maintain the status quo, especially from beneficiaries, personal risks, including persecution and violence, balancing spiritual responsibilities with social activism, maintaining a prophetic voice while also being a unifying figure, etc.

Despite these challenges, many Priests continue to speak and act with a commitment to faith and justice. Fr. Godfrey Nzamujo founded the Songhay Center in Benin to promote permaculture. Despite facing many challenges, including political control and threats from those who opposed his work, Fr. Nzamujo's efforts have changed countless lives and provided a model for sustainable development across Africa.

Opportunities

Despite these challenges, there are many opportunities for Catholic Priests to make a significant impact on justice in Nigeria. One such opportunity is increased awareness and commitment to justice in the Church. Documents such as *Rerum Novarum and Sollicitudo Rei Socialis* demonstrate the Church's responsibility to defend the poor and needy. Pope John II John Paul said in *Sollicitudo Rei Socialis*: "Solidarity is not a vague feeling or sadness for the suffering of many near and far. On the contrary, it is a strong will and decision of devotion towards good people" (Sollicitudo Rei Socialis, 38).

The rise of technology and social media has provided pastors with a powerful platform to raise awareness of injustice in society and encourage change. Social media can amplify the voices of social justice advocates, reach a wider audience, and foster a sense of international solidarity. These digital media are compatible with the missionary work of the Church and promote social justice in new ways.

Another opportunity lies in the Church's integration of schools, hospitals, and social services. These schools can address social inequality and improve people's lives. By incorporating social justice lessons into curricula and programs, churches can teach and inspire future generations to fight for justice.

Collaboration with other religious and religious organisations is also an important opportunity. The Church's commitment to dialogue and cooperation fosters partnerships that provide the benefits of social justice, as expressed in *A Light for All Peoples*: "The Church is sent to all peoples in all times and places, it is not exclusive, does not single out anyone. These partnerships can provide resources and expertise to develop stronger responses to societal challenges. In addition, the spiritual and moral wealth of the Church provides a solid basis for solving justice problems. Biblical principles such as the call to love one's neighbour (Matthew 22:39) and to seek justice (Isaiah 1:17) provide ongoing guidance for pastors. Christ's teachings about the poor and oppressed provide powerful examples that pastors can follow in their ministry.

Finally, the participation of increasing numbers of worshipers provides greater opportunities for justice. Lay people bring different skills and perspectives that can fulfil the job of a Priest. Encouraging marginalised people to participate in social justice projects not only demonstrates the authority of the Church but also fosters a sense of community cooperation.

In summary, while Catholic Priests in Nigeria face serious challenges in their work to achieve justice, there are many opportunities to make a significant impact. By applying the Church's teachings, using new technologies, and collaborating with other organisations, Priests can solve injustices affecting their communities. A commitment to justice and peace, rooted in the Bible and supported by the tradition of the Church, offers hope for a just society.

The Priest and Grassroots Interfaith

Grassroots interfaith dialogue is about building relationships with people of different faiths through community integration. This form of communication creates harmony and understanding, reduces stress and promotes harmony. Priests are uniquely positioned to lead these efforts because they are respected in the community and committed to social justice. The Bible calls for communication and understanding between different groups. The book of James says, *"How will it benefit the brethren if they confess their faith, but have no works. Can that faith save him?"* (James 2:14). Faith is manifested through actions that promote peace and justice, including religious cooperation.

Church documents also encourage unity. *Nostra Aetate,* the Declaration of the Second Vatican Council on Relations Between the Church and Non-Christians, emphasises the importance of dialogue and cooperation between people of different faiths. He states, "The Church condemns any discrimination or harassment against people because of race, colour, lifestyle or religion because this is contrary to the point of view of Jesus" (Nostra Aetate, 5). The document encourages Catholics to dialogue and work together with people of other faiths to achieve justice and peace.

A good way for Priests to participate in public communion is to attend or participate in community meetings that bring together people of different faiths. These activities may include community service projects, religious discussions, or cultural exchanges. Through these activities, Priests and their communities can build bridges and promote understanding and respect.

Pastors can help reduce ignorance and prejudice by educating congregations about other faiths and the importance of interfaith dialogue. This educational role is important in developing a culture of respect and understanding in society.

Proverbs says, *"A fool believes all things, but a wise man watches his steps"* (Proverbs 14:15). This highlights the importance of knowledge and thinking that can help us understand other religions and promote religious dialogue.

Grassroots interfaith work also includes efforts to solve social problems. For example, pastors can work with leaders of other faiths to solve problems in their communities, such as poverty, education, and health care. By working together on these issues, they can demonstrate the benefits of interfaith cooperation and build stronger and more resilient communities. The story of the Good Samaritan (Luke 10:25-37) provides a good biblical example of cooperation and compassion. In this parable, Jesus shows the importance of helping others, regardless of their origins or religion. Pastors can use this story to encourage their congregations to collaborate in faith and see the value in working for good with people of different faiths.

In addition to these activities and counselling, Priests can encourage religious dialogue through personal relationships. By forming friendships with leaders and members of other churches, pastors can model the type of relationships and cooperation they want to see in their congregations. These personal relationships can also form the basis for resolving conflicts and misunderstandings that may arise between different religious groups.

Religious debates are not free from difficulties. Differences in beliefs and practices sometimes lead to misunderstandings or conflicts. However, these challenges can be overcome with patience, openness, and a commitment to mutual respect. *The Gaudium et Spes* document of the Second Vatican Council emphasises the importance of understanding and cooperation in a pluralistic world. "By the very fact of creation," he said, "every human being is called to enter into relationships with others and create a human world" (Gaudium et Spes, 23). The literature supports Catholics viewing dialogue as an extension of their faith and a way to contribute to social harmony.

In Nigerian society, where religious diversity is a reality, the role of Priests in facilitating dialogue is particularly important. Priests can help build a peaceful and just society by encouraging public understanding and cooperation. This work not only demonstrates their faith but is also a good way to deal with the problems facing society.

CHAPTER V

The Digital Age and the Call to Authentic Witnessing

The digital age has revolutionised the Church's ability to reach a global audience. Social media platforms, websites, and streaming services allow the Church to share the Gospel message far beyond traditional geographic boundaries. Pope Francis has emphasised the importance of engaging with digital media to spread the Christian message, stating, "The internet can offer magnificent opportunities for evangelization if used with competence and a clear awareness of its strengths and weaknesses" (Francis, 2014).

As a member of the Catholic community in Nigeria, the digital age has profoundly influenced my experience of faith. The ability to connect with Catholics around the world through social media and online forums has enriched my understanding of the universal Church. Virtual access to the Vatican's archives and educational resources has deepened my theological knowledge and spiritual growth. Priests of contemporary times cannot risk not being tech-savvy and grounded in basic skills to aid in using digital space to maximise witnessing to the Gospel values and truth.

The digital age has transformed the connection between Catholic Priests and their communities in Nigeria. Online platforms provide powerful tools for evangelization, social engagements and pastoral care, allowing Priests to reach the faithful wherever they are. It is important to be open and transparent. However, pastors must approach the digital space with integrity and respect for privacy and dignity. The Catechism of the Catholic Church addresses this issue by emphasising the need to respect the fundamental rights of all people (CCC 1935). The digital age presents unprecedented opportunities for the Catholic Church to evangelize, educate, and build communities.

By embracing digital tools while addressing the associated challenges, the Church can continue to fulfill her mission in a rapidly changing world. The principles of Catholic social teaching provide a valuable framework for navigating the ethical complexities of the digital realm, ensuring that technology serves the common good and promotes human dignity.

While counting the gains in the use of digital media and space for evangelization and outreach, care must be taken, and its distractions and superficiality must not be taken for granted. The constant flow of information and the nature of social media can lead to distraction and superficial engagement with important issues. The Church must find ways to encourage deeper reflection and meaningful interaction in the digital space.

Pope Francis' Twitter account, @Pontifex, is a prime example of how the Church is using digital media for evangelization. With millions of followers across multiple languages, the Pope's tweets reach a global audience, offering messages of hope, prayer, and guidance. During the COVID-19 pandemic, many parishes worldwide adopted live-streamed Masses and virtual communities. This adaptation ensured that believers could continue to participate in the liturgy and maintain a sense of community despite physical distancing measures.

The Rise of Digital Ministries

The digital age has created unprecedented opportunities for the Catholic Church to expand her influence. As Pope Francis stated in his message for the 48th World Communication Day, "The Internet, in particular, has great potential for meeting and unity. It is truly a beautiful thing, a gift from God" (Francis, 2014). The endorsement of senior Church leaders not only follows the trend of digital platforms but also encourages pastors and religious leaders to explore these media as a good tool for preaching the Gospel. In today's world, digital transformation has changed the way society interacts, works, and, most importantly, worships. The shift to the digital world has had a profound impact on the work of the Catholic Church, especially in Nigeria, where the rapid adoption of technology has provided new opportunities for media and community development.

This rise in digital ministries became prominent during the COVID-19 pandemic lockdown. The lockdown was an eye-opener to many around the world. Physical gatherings were forbidden and restricted, so many people sought out an alternative to continue to foster unity in their various communities. While these digital tools have always been present even before the lockdown, they became more useful during that period, and many who were not aware of them became more aware and learned to embrace them. And so, different organisations began to hold their programs online and connect with members in any part of the world, and even long after the lockdown ended, churches continued to maximise the use of digital tools in the propagation of the Gospel.

In Nigeria, where mobile devices and Internet access are rapidly becoming widespread, digital work has enabled churches to connect with the community geographically and economically. It allows for the evangelization of those who cannot attend church services in person due to distance, health, or financial reasons. Platforms like social media, podcasts, and YouTube channels are forums for sharing God's word. The integration of technology into the preaching of the Gospel marks the transformation of the evangelism of the early Church. In Acts 1:8, Jesus told His disciples, "*But you will receive power when the Holy Spirit comes upon you, and you will be my witnesses in Jerusalem, in Judea and Samaria, and to the ends of the earth.*" Today, digital tools enable churches to work beyond the physical.

The main benefit of digital work is the Church's ability to reach believers who might otherwise be excluded due to one reason or the other and connect them to the many online prayers, Bible studies and digital activities for spiritual and social development. By effectively using social media, churches can address today's issues, answer questions, and provide spiritual guidance in an environment that engages young people. This partnership is necessary to maintain the Church's relevance in a rapidly changing world. Pope Francis' Apostolic Exhortation Evangelii Gaudium emphasises the importance of communication in the media today: "The changes taking place in the media and information technology represent a great and exciting challenge; how can we use new energy and competitive thinking to encourage organisations to be creative and innovative in their digital advertising?" While useful, one of the challenges of working digitally is ensuring the authenticity and depth of online conversations, where sometimes the depth of personal conversations and face-to-face conversations is not available. Therefore, digital care should complement rather than replace traditional care.

Similarly, while digital technology offers numerous benefits, there is also the issue of digital divide. Not all communities have equal access to the Internet and digital tools. The Church must address this inequality to ensure that all believers can benefit from digital evangelization and pastoral care. An additional challenge the Church faces in the digital age is maintaining the authenticity of her message. The fast-paced nature of digital communication can sometimes lead to misinterpretations or the spread of misinformation. The Church must strive to ensure that her digital presence accurately reflects her teachings and values.

Moral judgment also plays an important role in digital studies. Churches must use these tools responsibly to ensure that the content shared is accurate, respectful, and consistent with the teachings of Jesus. In his message on the 45th World Communication Day, Pope Benedict XVI warned, "New technologies must be used to promote human dignity and goodness." The report underlines the need for churches to uphold ethical standards in their digital activities.

In summary, the use of technology in evangelism offers significant opportunities for the Catholic Church in Nigeria to expand her reach, engage the faithful, and respond to today's challenges. Through the use of digital platforms, churches can fulfil their mission, social outreach, and spiritual leadership in an ever-changing world. This carefully managed digital transformation promises to advance the mission of the Church and ensure that the message of love and hope reaches every corner of society.

Accepting the call to digital ministry can also be supported by Scripture. In the Book of Acts, we see the ancient Church using modern technology (paper and letters) to spread the Gospel throughout the region (Acts 15:20 -21). Likewise, today's digital tools can be thought of as modern letters that spread the message of Jesus Christ around the world through digital networks.

Ethics must also be considered as the Church explores the digital frontier. In his 45th World Communication Day message, Pope Benedict XVI reminded that "New technologies should not be used in reality" (Benedict XVI, 2011). Digital leaders must strive for a true, honest and transparent presentation of the Catholic faith and not fall for the superficiality often seen in the media.

Theologically, digital ministry should reflect the conviction of our faith – the incarnation of God (John 1:14). It should embody God's Word in digital form, be understandable and relevant, and at the same time preserve its divine content. The rise of digital businesses in Nigeria represents the intersection of religion and technology. It provides the Catholic Church with effective tools for evangelization in today's world, enabling it to evangelize widely. As this ministry grows, it must seek the stability of the Gospel and adapt to new challenges, remaining at the centre of Church leadership. By careful and thoughtful use of digital tools based on Scripture and Church teaching, the Catholic Church in Nigeria can fulfil her mission here in the new digital age, reaching all parts of the country and beyond to educate people digitally.

Engaging the Faithful Through Social Media

The digital revolution has changed many aspects of life today, including the way people communicate, work and worship. For the Catholic Church, especially in Nigeria, the rise of social media provides an unprecedented opportunity to engage with Christians all over the world and spread the Gospel.

In the past, the Catholic Church used traditional methods such as sermons, printed materials, and face-to-face meetings to communicate with believers. Although these methods are important, the emergence of social media offers new ways to participate. As Pope Francis stated, "The Internet can give everyone more opportunities for meeting and sharing, and that is a good thing; it is a gift from God" (Francis, 2014). Social media platforms such as Facebook, Twitter, Instagram and YouTube have become important tools for reaching believers, especially young people who spend a lot of time online.

The Use of Social Media for Evangelization

The use of social media for evangelism is consistent with the Church's mission to spread the Gospel to all corners of the world. In Acts 1:8, Jesus said to his disciples, *"But you will receive power when the Holy Spirit has come upon you, and you will be my witnesses in Jerusalem and in all Judea and Samaria and to the ends of the earth."* Today, social media is a daily witness and allows the Church to reach far beyond the physical. In Nigeria, access to the Internet is widespread and social media allows the Church to connect across borders. It allows the Gospel to be preached to those who cannot attend church services in person due to distance, health, or financial constraints. For example, during the COVID-19 pandemic, many Nigerian churches began streaming liturgies and other religious services online to enable the faithful to participate in worship in times of lockdown when public gatherings were prohibited. This change not only maintains a sense of community but also demonstrates the Church's ability to respond to today's problems with new solutions.

Building Online Communities

Social media is more than a tool for spreading the word; it is also a place where communities can be built and sustained. Online prayer groups, Bible classes, and virtual workouts provide opportunities for spiritual and social growth. These digital gatherings can complement traditional church events and provide a sense of belonging and support for individuals who feel alone.

Apostle Paul's use of letters to communicate with the early believers in various parts of the world may be considered as a forerunner of today's digital communication. In his letters, Paul gives guidance, encouragement, and fellowship to scattered believers (Acts 15:20-21). Likewise, social media allows Priests and leaders to provide spiritual support and guidance to their communities, promoting unity and shared faith.

Engaging Young People through Social Media

Social media is a hub for the youth, and we must engage them more by meeting them where they are. One of the main benefits of social media is its ability to attract young people. Many young people today prefer to communicate and engage with the Church online through digital platforms. By effectively using social media, churches can address today's issues, answer questions, and provide spiritual guidance in a way that appeals to young people.

Pope Francis, in his Apostolic Exhortations *Evangelii Gaudium*, emphasises the importance of collaborating with young people in evangelistic work, "The revolution in communication requires new energy and thought in the dissemination of the Gospel" (Francis, 2013). Social media is a powerful and interactive tool for this participation; by providing a platform, it allows the Church to take part in the digital life of young people, providing an opportunity for connection and community for the Church, but also creating solutions to problems. However, it is necessary to note that digital communication can sometimes lack the personal touch and intimacy of face-to-face interaction that is so important to pastoral care. Therefore, the role of the media should be to support rather than replace the knowledge of the discipline.

Summarily, the theological basis for the use of social media in evangelism can be traced back to the early churches where modern communication methods were used. The Congregation for the Doctrine of the Faith "Inter Mirifica" of the Second Vatican Council stated the Church's duty to use the media as follows: "The Church recognises that the media can be useful to humanity if necessary" (Vatican II, 1963). This document provides easy support for participating on digital platforms and encourages churches to deliver salvation in a modern way.

The principle of acculturation, in which the Gospel should be incorporated into different cultures, also supports the use of social media. Just as early missionaries adapted their approach to the culture they encountered, today's churches must adapt to digital culture. By doing so, one can communicate the timeless truth of the Gospel in a way that will resonate with today's listeners.

Many Archdioceses and dioceses in Nigeria have achieved social success through their work. The diocese maintains a social media page that offers daily inspiration, Bible verses and teachings and reaches a diverse audience that extends well beyond the community. For example, the Diocese of Lagos has a strong presence online with social media partners sharing news, events and spiritual reflections. This digital engagement not only increases Christian awareness but also strengthens the sense of connection and community. Likewise, pastors and religious leaders use social media to share their sermons, thoughts, and teachings to reach people who cannot attend Church regularly.

Preserving the Deposit of the Faith

As the Church moves into digital frontiers, it is important to stay true to the faith. Theological considerations are necessary to ensure that messages broadcast by the media remain faithful to the Church's teachings. This involves following the teachings set forth in important documents such as *Lumen Gentium and Nostra Aetate*, which address the role of the Church today and her relationship to the world. Digital media should reflect the incarnation aspect of faith – God became man (John 1:14). Media must follow God's Word in digital form and be accessible and relevant while preserving her sacred content. This approach ensures that the Church's digital presence remains at her theological foundation, providing an authentic and reliable witness to the Gospel.

The Catholic Church in Nigeria can fulfil her mission in the digital age by exercising caution and using the media responsibly, as Scripture and the Church teach. This approach not only expands the Church's reach but also improves her ability to support the faith of millions of people around the world. By maintaining the balance between digital and traditional work, the Church can ensure that the message of love and hope reaches every corner of society, builds trust, and engages with society.

Challenges and Opportunities in the Digital Space

In an era of rapid growth, the Catholic Church faces unique challenges and opportunities in the digital sphere. Integrating digital tools has revolutionised the way the Church reaches believers and media and supports the community. While these technologies offer unprecedented opportunities, they also present significant challenges that require thoughtful responses and strategies.

Reaching More People

One of the greatest opportunities of the digital age is the Church's ability to reach a broader audience. With the advent of the Internet, social media platforms, and mobile technology, the Church can spread her message to people all over the world. Speaking about the potential of this tool, Pope Francis said: "The Internet, in particular, has great potential for meeting and unity. This is truly a very good thing, a gift from God" (Francis, 2014). Digital projects allow congregations to share the Gospel, preach, and provide spiritual support to those who cannot reach them due to geography, economy or communication.

Youth Engagement

Digital ministry has also opened up new ways to engage with the youth. Young people are often at the forefront of using new technologies and spend a lot of time online. Churches can engage youths in their messages using social media, podcasts, and YouTube channels. This path helps solve their problems, provides spiritual guidance and makes Church teachings understandable and relevant. As Jesus said, *"Let the little children come to me, and do not hinder them, for theirs is the kingdom of heaven"* (Matthew 19:14). Engage with youth through digital means to ensure they feel included and valued by the church community.

Digital Divide

The transition to digital work is not without challenges. An important issue is the digital divide. There is a significant difference in Internet usage between urban and rural areas in Nigeria.

Although most urban areas have strong telecommunications, rural areas lag behind, limiting access to digital media and lack of technical know-how on how to operate digital devices. This distribution can further exacerbate existing inequalities, leaving rural communities underserved. Churches must find ways to close this gap, perhaps by offering offline programs, creating mobile outreach sites, and partnering with technology companies to improve online access in underdeveloped areas.

Maintaining Originality and Depth

Another challenge is maintaining originality and depth in online interactions. While digital platforms provide convenience and accessibility, they can sometimes lack the personal touch and depth of a community where face-to-face interaction is common. The sacrament is the foundation of the Catholic faith; it must be physical and cannot be reproduced in digital format. As stated in the Apostolic Exhortation *Evangelii Gaudium*, "The digital world can be a circle of people, a network of people, not wires" (Francis, 2013). Churches must ensure that digital work complements rather than replaces in-person care and community building.

Promoting Ethical Behaviour

Ethical judgment also plays a vital role in the digital environment. Anonymity and disruption on the Internet can lead to the spread of misinformation and unethical practices. Pope Benedict XVI emphasised the need for justice in digital communications and warned, "New technologies must be used to promote human dignity and individual well-being." The Church must maintain an ethical standard and ensure that what is shared online is accurate, respectful and consistent with her guidelines. This responsibility includes protecting the privacy and security of believers who interact with the Church through digital platforms.

Adapting to Technological Change

Rapid change requires the Church to change and innovate constantly. Being in the digital age means supporting new technology and processes. This change can be seen as part of the Church's broader mission to "*be of the world, but not of the world*" (John 17:14-15). By encouraging innovation, the Church can find new ways to fulfill her mission of evangelism and ministry while preserving her core values and traditions.

Collaboration

The digital age also offers opportunities for collaboration. Churches can use digital platforms to share resources and best practices and support each other in their work. Online communities and forums provide an environment where clergy and laypeople can exchange ideas, find ideas, and collaborate on projects. This online approach can increase the efficiency of work and promote a sense of unity in the global Catholic community.

Responding to Current Issues

Additionally, digital tools can enhance the Church's ability to respond to today's issues and problems quickly. For example, during the COVID-19 pandemic, many churches turned to online services, online prayer groups, and virtual services to continue their activities despite closures and different precautions. These digital changes not only allow the Church to manage her own life but also demonstrate her ability to innovate in the face of challenges.

Further Education and Training

Integrating digital tools also requires ongoing education and training of clergy and leaders. Understanding how to use these technologies effectively, overcome potential barriers, and leverage their full potential is crucial to successful digital operations. Training, online learning, and collaborative learning can provide Church leaders with the knowledge and skills they need to thrive in the digital age.

Advocacy and Public Discourse

The digital space provides a platform for organisations to engage in public debate and advocate for justice. By participating in online discussions, churches can raise awareness of important issues such as poverty, inequality, and human rights. This initiative is based on the Church's mission to *"bring good news to the poor... and freedom to the oppressed"* (Luke 4:18). Digital platforms offer a powerful way to amplify the Church's voice and promote social justice.

Balance of Collaboration with Spirituality

The widespread use of social media has the potential to weaken the outlook and perspective of the Catholic faith by fostering a culture of distraction, superficiality, and instant gratification. The Second Vatican Council' Inter Mirifica' says, "Communication in society should serve the human heart and promote the common good" (Vatican II, 1963). Churches should encourage responsible and mindful use of digital technology by encouraging a balanced approach that combines digital engagement with deep spirituality and reflection.

The digital age brings challenges and opportunities to the Catholic Church in Nigeria. By embracing digital tools and platforms, churches can expand their reach, engage a broader audience, and respond to today's challenges. However, this digital transformation needs to be done carefully to complement the documentation of traditional studies, support standards of practice, and promote people's well-being. As the church journeys to this place of power, she must remain steadfast in her mission to preach the Gospel, serve the community, and uphold the dignity of all people.

Recommendable Best Practices for Online Ministry

In today's digital age, the Catholic Church has an unprecedented opportunity to reach both believers and non-believers through online media. As technology continues to evolve, pastors and religious leaders must adopt best practices for efficient and effective online ministry. The Internet and social media have become an important part of people's lives, providing new ways of communication and pastoral care. Online preaching, if done well, can reach a wide audience, provide spiritual support, and create a sense of community among Christians.

However, it is still a problem that needs to be handled carefully in terms of ethics and culture. Looking at the best practices for engaging online in a way that is effective and faithful to the teachings of the Catholic Church, we have:

Authenticity and Transparency

Authenticity is a foundation that guides the actions of Catholic Priests in Nigeria in online preaching. Upholding this principle requires a relationship and transparency that reflects the teachings and values of the Catholic Church. The important thing here is that the person expresses his/her own honest opinion and is not influenced or deceived. As Matthew 5:37 explains, *"Let your yes be yes and your no be no; anything more than this comes from evil."*

Religion and Privacy in Nigeria

The Canon of the Catholic Church emphasises the protection of the dignity of all people. Respect for privacy and dignity is essential in online activities. This includes obtaining consent before sharing personal information, using caution when discussing sensitive topics, and protecting the privacy of those seeking pastoral care.

Christian syncretism in the Nigerian social context faces formidable challenges that must overcome the complexity of traditional religions and the influence of the country. Nigerian Christians integrate indigenous culture into their worship, creating a uniquely Nigerian Christianity (Peel, 2000). However, this combination requires a little balance. Nigerian Christians must overcome traditional religious practices that often oppress local culture and religion. Despite these challenges, Christianity in Nigeria has flourished, incorporating various forms of culture while retaining her core teachings.

Additionally, the Church's message of privacy and dignity resonates with Nigerians and reflects our shared commitment to care for and respect the worth of all people. Jesus has compassion and respect for everyone, regardless of their life and background, and He shows this in His relationships. Self-respect and dignity are important in online advertising because they reflect the values of Christianity. In Nigeria, this reverence is linked to the country's rich heritage and highlights the importance of respecting people's symbols and experiences.

Creating an Online Presence

In the digital age, the online presence of the Catholic Church in Nigeria is not only about sharing information but also about socialising and building a sense of community. Online approval starts with the tone and content of your message. Words of love, hope and compassion should be encouraged, and words that could cause separation or pain should be avoided. St. Paul's letter to the Ephesians (4:29) teaches that words have the power to build or destroy, and it is good to use words to build and be kind to those who hear them.

Maintaining a positive online presence includes communicating with others respectfully and understandingly. This means listening to the concerns and feelings of others and responding with understanding and compassion, even if their opinions are different from your own. It also means being mindful of the impact our words and actions can have on others. This is especially true in online environments where discussions can be heated or contradictory.

In addition to the content of the message, the communication environment also plays a vital role in creating a good image online. Photos, videos, and other multimedia can help you convey your message more effectively and efficiently. However, it is important to ensure that the use of this information is ethical and in accordance with Church teachings.

Creating a good image online requires effort and attention. Sharing nice words is not enough; we ought to try to follow the words in our conversations with others. By spreading messages of love, hope, and compassion online, we can help create a better, more supportive online community that reflects the values of the Catholic Church.

Provide Pastoral Care and Support

The online ministry offers a unique opportunity for Catholic Priests in Nigeria to provide care and support to those unable to use traditional religion. This may include online services, prayer services, and spiritual guidance. These interactions should be filled with compassion, understanding, and a genuine desire to help, echoing Pope Francis' words about the usefulness of the Internet for meeting and sharing. Pastoral care in the digital age requires Priests to participate and attend to the needs of online communities. This will include responding quickly to messages and comments and actively seeking support and encouragement. Through action, Priests can demonstrate the Church's commitment to caring for all members of society, online and offline.

In summary, the online ministry provides Catholic Priests in Nigeria with powerful tools for evangelism and pastoral care. By developing an effective online presence, providing care and support, and integrating Christianity into Nigerian society, pastors can engage believers and non-believers alike and spread the message of God's love and mercy in the digital age.

CHAPTER VI

The Dynamics of Faith in Contemporary Nigeria

Nigeria, often referred to as the "Giant of Africa," is a nation marked by her diverse cultural, ethnic, and religious landscape. This diversity significantly shapes the dynamics of faith within the country. The Catholic Church, amidst this vibrant and sometimes volatile environment, faces unique challenges and opportunities. This chapter examines the intricate dynamics of faith in contemporary Nigeria and how Catholics live out their spiritual lives amidst social, political, and cultural complexities.

Nigeria is home to a multitude of religious beliefs, with Islam and Christianity being the predominant faiths. This pluralistic environment fosters a rich tapestry of religious expression but also presents challenges in maintaining interfaith harmony. A complex interplay of cultural, social, and political factors shapes the dynamics of faith in contemporary Nigeria. The intersection of faith and culture is a daily reality.

The Catholic Church, with her rich tradition of social teaching and commitment to justice, plays a pivotal role in addressing these challenges and seizing opportunities for positive change.

The Church's teachings provide a moral compass and a source of strength amidst the country's challenges. Witnessing the Church's role in advocating for justice and providing essential services is inspiring. However, the journey is not without its hurdles, particularly in navigating interfaith tensions and engaging the youth. By engaging with the digital age, advocating for social justice, and fostering interfaith dialogue, the Church continues to be a beacon of hope and a force for good in Nigeria.

Religion in Nigeria is not static but a powerful force that influences daily life. It is embedded in culture, tradition, and social rules and shapes the worldview of individuals and communities. The Catholic Church, the main religious institution in Nigeria, has played an important role in the development of the faith. The Church provides spiritual guidance and support through her teachings and sacraments to help Christians cope with the challenges of today's Nigerian society. Nigeria's religious dynamics reflect the country's rich religious diversity and cultural heritage and highlight the importance of religion in the lives of Nigerians.

Commercialisation of the Christian Faith and Rise in Pentecostalism

The religious landscape in Nigeria has changed significantly in recent years. These changes were caused by the increasing commercialisation of Christianity and the rise of Pentecostalism. These trends had a significant impact on Christianity and the role of Catholic Priests in the country. Understanding these changes requires examining the events that led to these changes and their effects on Christians.

The economy of Christianity refers to the structure in which economic forces increase religion and belief. Some leaders have turned the Church into a business and are treating it like one. This phenomenon is reflected in the growth of megachurches and the commercialisation of religion and religious services. These changes are not just cosmetic; they undermine the foundations of belief and practice.

Pentecostalism represents a strong and powerful branch of Christianity that emphasises the righteousness of the Holy Spirit, spiritual gifts such as "speaking in tongues" and the way of prophecy, and a relationship with Jesus Christ. The number of Pentecostal churches in Nigeria has grown and is still on the rise; they have attracted millions of followers with their worship services, leadership, and promises of miracles and prosperity.

The development of Pentecostalism in Nigeria can be traced to the early 20th century. However, the exponential growth in recent years has been particularly striking and difficult to ignore. This growth has been driven by many factors, including the attractiveness of knowledge, the charisma of leaders of many Pentecostal Churches, subscriptions to emotionalism, poverty and Nigeria's ability to adapt to today's socio-economic reality. Pentecostal churches provide a sense of community, hope, and support to members who often face financial problems and poverty.

The commercialisation of the Christian religion is linked to the rise of Pentecostalism. Many Pentecostal churches have adopted business practices to stimulate growth and expand their influence. This includes the use of media and technology to reach a wider audience, create business opportunities, and inform members' financial growth. These practices are sometimes criticised for their emphasis on material wealth and progress rather than spiritual and moral development.

The Catholic Church, with her rich tradition and deep religious foundations, faces unique challenges and opportunities in the evolving theological environment. Catholic Priests in Nigeria must respond to these changes by remaining faithful to their responsibilities of pastoral care, evangelisation, and social justice. We need to find a way to reach believers who are more impressed by the promises of prosperity and miracles provided by the Pentecostal Church.

One of the main duties of Catholic Priests is to solve the problems of believers regarding religious affairs. This requires an analysis of the importance of market forces that influence religious beliefs and create false beliefs. Pastors should emphasise the importance of spiritual justice, social justice, and evangelism in their ministries. They should also provide clear instructions on the difference between true beliefs and beliefs aimed at increasing wealth.

Jesus' cleansing of the temple (Matthew 21:12–13) is a powerful warning about the dangers of works in religious practice. In this verse, Jesus expelled the money changers and merchants from the temple and declared, "*My house will be called a house of prayer, but you have turned it into a thieves' cave.*" The teachings of the early Church and the documents of the Church provide a good insight into the relationship between religion and business. For example, the "*Lumen Gentium*" document of the Second Vatican Council emphasises that the mission of the Church is to serve the spiritual and temporal needs of the same people without compromising the integrity of her words. It calls for a commitment to social justice and relationships, as opposed to the personal and material interests of commercial religion.

Catholic Priests can also draw on the Church's rich tradition of leadership to find solutions to the economic crisis that has driven many Nigerians to Pentecostal churches. The Church's social teachings, expressed in documents such as *Rerum Novarum and*

Centesimus Annus, provide a basis for promoting justice, human dignity, and goodness. By addressing the root causes of poverty and inequality, churches can provide a more effective and efficient response to the needs of believers.

Collaboration with believers interested in Pentecostalism requires compassionate and understanding leadership. Catholic Priests should attend to the spiritual and emotional needs of their congregation and provide support and guidance regarding their lifestyle. This includes creating spaces for worship and fellowship, fostering a sense of community and belonging, and providing opportunities for spiritual growth and development. At the same time, Catholic Priests must carefully follow the teachings and morals of the Church. This includes addressing false beliefs or persecution that may occur in the Pentecostal context while also acknowledging the true spiritual knowledge and understanding that Pentecostal Christians bring to believers around the world. Dialogue and collaboration with Pentecostal leaders and communities can foster understanding and respect while also providing opportunities for shared witness and accountability.

The rise of Pentecostalism also forced Catholic Priests to renew their missionary work. This includes using modern technology and media to reach a broader audience while preserving the integrity and depth of the Catholic faith. Social media, online platforms, and other digital tools can become powerful tools for evangelism, religious education, and community building. However, to ensure that they are stronger without weak faith, their use must be guided by a clear understanding of the Church's mission and importance.

In summary, the commercialisation of Christianity and the rise of Pentecostalism have created challenges and opportunities for Catholic Priests in Nigeria. By responding to these standards with confidence, pastoral thought, and new ideas, Priests can help believers come to a more accurate and better understanding of the Christian faith. This requires commitment to the teaching of the Bible, the rich culture of the Church, and the needs of those in charge to ensure that the Church remains a beacon of hope, truth, and justice in a changing world.

The Impacts of Pentecostalism on Catholicism

The religious landscape in Nigeria has changed significantly in the last few decades. One of the most significant changes was the rise of Pentecostalism. The movement had a huge impact on the Catholic Church, not only in terms of what the faith is like but also in how the Church interacts with her followers and the power of society. Understanding these influences requires a closer look at the dynamics of Pentecostalism and Catholicism, especially in the Nigerian context.

Changes in Worship Traditions

Pentecostalism gained popularity in Nigeria and is characterised by good worship, personal experience with the Holy Spirit, and the promise of success. This development created problems and opportunities for the Catholic Church and made it reflect on her practices and methods. One of the most important effects of the Pentecostal movement on Catholicism is the change in liturgical styles. Pentecostal services are known for their powerful music, sustained prayers, and sermons. This contrasts with the more traditional and liturgical methods of the Catholic Church, which are ritualistic, solemn and traditional. That's why many Catholics, especially young people, are attracted to Pentecostal churches, where they feel a direct and personal connection to their faith, and this may be partly the reason for the migration of a handful of the young from the Church. The Catholic Church should reform to include important points in worship while maintaining the liturgy of the Church. Participation in these movements is increasing, especially among young people looking for a spiritual connection.

Spiritual Knowledge

The rise of Pentecostalism also emphasised the importance of spiritual knowledge. Pentecostalism places great emphasis on man's relationship with God, often expressed through rhetoric such as divination, healing, and divination. This emphasis on personal spirituality has led many Catholics to seek a deeper understanding of their faith. In response, the Catholic Church saw the growth of a charismatic revival movement within the Catholic Church. These movements encourage Catholics to enjoy the blessings of the Holy Spirit while remaining faithful to Catholic teachings and traditions. This led to a renewed emphasis on personal prayer, spiritual retreats, and other activities that encouraged direct contact with God.

Prosperity Theology and its Influence

Additionally, the Gospel message preached by many Pentecostal churches has had a great impact on Catholicism in Nigeria. This belief, which equates faith with material well-being and health, appeals to many Nigerians facing economic difficulties. The allure of success and miracles has led some Catholics to question the Church's teachings on suffering, sacrifice, and social justice. The Catholic Church must reaffirm her teaching on the value of suffering, happiness, and the pursuit of justice. The Church draws on a rich culture and social teachings that emphasise spirituality and unity rather than the promise of Gospel prosperity. This is a new version of Jesus' teachings about wealth and poverty.

Biblical and Theological Foundations

Biblical references play an important role in this discussion. For example, Jesus' teaching in Matthew 6:19-21 instructs believers, *"Put up treasures in heaven, where moth do not destroy, and where thieves do not steal for where your treasure is, there your heart will also be."* Additionally, the parable of the rich fool in Luke 12:16-21 warns against focusing on material things. These verses challenge the prosperity Gospel's emphasis on worldly wealth and shift the focus to spiritual wealth. The second document of the Vatican Council, *Lumen Gentium*, clearly states that the mission of the Church is to meet the spiritual and physical needs of people without harming the teaching of the Church and calls for loyalty and devotion to humanity rather than personal gain (Lumen Gentium 8).

The Role of Catholic Priests

In response to the rise of Pentecostalism, Catholic Priests in Nigeria need to monitor and evangelize their pastors. They must meet the spiritual needs of their congregations while dealing with the global economic challenges facing their communities. This includes providing clarity and compassion regarding the daily lives of parishioners.

Distinguishing Catholicism from Pentecostal Practices

Catholicism and Pentecostalism are two significant branches of Christianity, each with its unique beliefs, practices, and traditions (Catechism of the Catholic Church, 1994). While they share some commonalities, such as a belief in the Trinity and the divinity of Jesus Christ (Catholic Church, 1994), they also have distinct differences that set them apart.

Ecclesiastical Hierarchy

The ecclesiastical structures of Catholicism and Pentecostalism stand in stark contrast, particularly in their organisational hierarchy and the distribution of authority. Understanding these differences sheds light on how each tradition functions and perceives its spiritual leadership.

Catholic Ecclesiastical Structure: The Catholic Church's hierarchy is deeply entrenched in tradition and history, reflecting a pyramid-like structure with the Pope at her zenith. Beneath him are the Cardinals, Bishops, Priests, and Deacons, each with distinct roles and responsibilities. This hierarchical setup finds its roots in the belief of apostolic succession, a doctrine asserting that the authority and spiritual gifts bestowed upon the apostles by Jesus have been transmitted through an unbroken line of succession to the present clergy (Lumen Gentium, 1964).

Pentecostal Approach: Conversely, Pentecostalism often embraces a more decentralised and egalitarian approach, emphasising the priesthood of all believers (1 Peter 2:5, 9-10). In this framework, there is a lesser emphasis on a rigid hierarchy and a greater emphasis on the empowerment of individual believers to engage in spiritual practices and exercise spiritual gifts. While some Pentecostal denominations may have leaders like pastors or elders, the overall structure tends to be more fluid and less formally structured compared to Catholicism.

Biblical Basis: The Catholic hierarchical structure finds support in various biblical passages and traditions. For example, Jesus' appointment of Peter as the rock upon which He would build His Church (Matthew 16:18-19) is often cited as the basis for the papacy. Similarly, the appointment of bishops and Priests can be traced back to the early Christian communities, where leaders were appointed to oversee and guide the faithful. In contrast,

Pentecostalism emphasises the priesthood of all believers, a concept derived from passages like 1 Peter 2:5, 9-10, which describes believers as a "royal priesthood" and a "holy nation." This emphasis on the priesthood of all believers underscores the idea that all Christians have direct access to God and can serve as spiritual leaders in their own right.

The ecclesiastical structures of Catholicism and Pentecostalism reflect their unique theological emphases and historical developments. While Catholicism is characterised by a hierarchical structure rooted in apostolic succession and tradition, Pentecostalism emphasises the priesthood of all believers, and it tends to take a more egalitarian and decentralised approach. Understanding these differences is essential for appreciating the diversity within Christianity and how different traditions approach spiritual leadership and authority.

Sacraments and Worship

Catholic emphasises on sacraments. The foundation of Catholic worship is the sacrament of life, deeply grounded in the belief that the sacrament is a product of innate grace produced by the divine grace of Christ's own signature. The Catechism of the Catholic Church (1994) defines the sacraments as signs of grace created by Christ and entrusted to the Church, through which divine life is given to us. Catholics believe that they receive God's grace through the sacraments, which strengthens their faith and helps them live according to the teachings of Christ. Catholicism recognises **seven sacraments: Baptism, Confirmation, Eucharist, Confession, Anointing of the Sick, Priesthood, and Marriage**. Each of these sacraments plays an important role in the life of Catholics and marks important moments of spiritual growth and devotion. For example, Baptism is seen as a gateway to the sacraments. Confirmation strengthens the believer, and the Eucharist is considered the beginning and end of what people believe.

Biblical Foundations

The foundation of the liturgy is found in the Bible; The basis for many things is found in the actions and teachings of Jesus. For example, the Eucharist was received at Christ's Last Supper with His disciples; here, He created the sacrament by distributing bread and wine to them and teaching them to do the same in His memory (Luke 22:14-20). Likewise, the sacrament of Baptism is based on Jesus' command to baptize all nations in the name of the Father, the Son, and the Holy Spirit (Matthew 28:19).

Pentecostalism in Knowledge and Gifts

In contrast, Pentecostalism places greater emphasis on the worship of God; this often results from the manifestation of spiritual gifts such as speech, prophecy, and healing. This is important in believing that the Holy Spirit inspires believers to live as believers and be good witnesses for Christ (1 Corinthians 12-14; Acts 2:1-4, 10: 44-47, 19:1-6).

In summary, Catholicism emphasises the sacraments as grace and spiritual health, while Pentecostalism emphasises the experience of worship and sharing spiritual gifts. Both traditions play an important role in the lives of Christians and inform their understanding of God and their relationship with Him.

Interpretation of Revelation

This means that for Catholics, teachings are derived not only from the Bible but also from the teachings of the early Church and the decisions of Church councils.

Catholicism views the Bible and tradition as the two primary sources of revelation, with the Magisterium (the teaching authority of the Church) responsible for interpreting and safeguarding the deposit of faith. The Catechism of the Catholic Church (1994) explains that the Magisterium, consisting of the Pope and the Bishops in communion with him, is entrusted with authentically interpreting the Word of God, whether written or handed down, so that it may shine forth as the perennial source of the Church's faith and the light of the human race. While the Bible is considered the inspired Word of God, tradition plays an important role in developing the Church's understanding of theology and ethics. This understanding is based on the belief that the Holy Spirit guides the Church in the interpretation of both Scripture and tradition, ensuring that the Church remains faithful to the teachings of Christ.

Pentecostals Emphasise Sola Scriptura

In contrast, Pentecostals tend to emphasise the principle of sola scriptura, whereby Christians interpret the Bible under the guidance of the Holy Spirit. This approach is based on scriptures such as 2 Timothy 3:16-17, which states that all Scripture is inspired by God and is useful for teaching, rebuking, correcting, and training in righteousness so that God's servants may be thoroughly equipped for every good work.

Biblical Fundamentals

Pentecostals believe that the Bible is the final authority on faith and practice and is sufficient to guide believers in their Christian walk. They emphasise the personal relationship between a believer and God, with the Holy Spirit playing a central role in illuminating the meaning of Scripture and guiding believers in their understanding.

In summary, Catholicism views Scripture and tradition as sources of revelation, interpretation, and religious authority, while

Pentecostalism tends to emphasise the authority of Scripture, which Christians interpret under the guidance of the Holy Spirit. These approaches illustrate the theological thought and practices of these traditions, highlighting their distinctiveness within the broader Christian faith.

Preserving Catholic Traditions in Modern Times

Preserving Catholic traditions is significant for maintaining the faith and identity of the Church. This section explores the importance of preserving Catholic traditions, the challenges posed by modern times, and strategies for preservation.

The Importance of Following Catholic Tradition

Catholic tradition is an essential part of the Church's identity and the foundation of her faith, leadership, and values. Deeply rooted in Scripture, the teachings of the early church fathers, and the Magisterium, these traditions play an important role in shaping the faith and identity of Catholics worldwide. Protecting these traditions doesn't just mean enforcing the law; It is about making the Church's heritage important to support and guide believers in their faith. The Catholic tradition is rooted in the Bible. Jesus sent His disciples, *"Make disciples of all nations, baptizing them in the name of the Father and of the Son and of the Holy Spirit, teaching them to observe all that I have commanded you…"* (Matthew 28:19-20). These commandments form the basis of many church traditions, including ordinances, liturgies, and moral teachings.

Influence of the Early Church Fathers

The teachings of the early Church fathers also played an important role in the formation of the Catholic tradition. Leaders such as St. Irenaeus defended the faith and doctrines against Heresies and became the basis of many Church's teachings. His writings, along with those of other early church fathers, continue to inspire and guide Catholic faith and practice today.

Preamble to the Episcopal Conference

The Episcopal Conference, founded by the Pope and his associated Bishops, plays an important role in the interpretation and preservation of the Catholic tradition. Documents such as "*Lumen Gentium*" (1964) emphasised the importance of tradition in the life of the Church, saying, "This tradition came from the apostles, established in the Church with the help of the Holy Spirit." The guidance of the Holy Spirit ensures that the Church's tradition remains true to her origins while adapting to the changes of the faithful.

Continuity and Unity

The preservation of Catholic tradition provides continuity with the past and creates stability and unity in the face of change. These traditions connect Catholics to their religious heritage and remind them of the sacrifices and struggles of those who came before them. They are also a source of unity that unites Catholics from different cultures and backgrounds in a single faith.

We remember that the importance of preserving the Catholic tradition cannot be ignored. These traditions are rooted in the Bible, the teachings of the early church fathers, and the traditions of the Church, and are necessary to keep the icon and fellowship together in the Church. By preserving these traditions, Catholics can ensure that the Church's rich heritage continues to support and guide the faithful.

The Contemporary Wars on Catholic Traditions

Secularism and Materialism

In today's world, secularism and materialism pose serious challenges to the preservation of Catholic customary law. Secularism promotes a worldview that excludes religious considerations from public life, leading to a decrease in respect for religious traditions and customs. Materialism, on the other hand, refers to the search for wealth and physical comfort rather than spiritual and moral concerns that may lead to non-compliance with religious obligations (Pope John Paul II, Veritatis Splendor, 1993, p. 25).

Globalisation and Cultural Homogenization

Globalisation promotes the global spread of ideas, values, and practices, leading to cultural homogenization. While this created opportunities for dialogue and understanding between different cultures, it also led to the extinction of certain cultures and religious practices. The influence of foreign cultures can lead to a lack of faith and culture, making it difficult for the Catholic tradition to maintain its uniqueness (Pope Benedict XVI, Caritas Veritas, 2011, p. 45).

Technological Developments

Although the use of technology provides many benefits, it has also created problems in terms of preserving the Catholic tradition. Advances in digital media and communications technology have changed the way people access and interact with information, including religious education. The rapid dissemination of ideas and information through digital platforms can lead to the spread of beliefs and practices that may impact or affect the Catholic tradition. Additionally, reliance on technology for religion, such as online worship, would diminish the importance of religious structures and communities (Redemtoris Missio, 1990, p. 75).

Diversity in the Church

The racial and religious diversity in the Catholic Church also causes problems in terms of preserving culture. As the Church expands into different regions and interacts with different cultures, it must resolve the conflict between maintaining her traditional teachings and practices and behaving according to the culture of her members. This difference can lead to disagreements in the Church over the interpretation and application of traditional teachings, making it difficult to practice unity and maintain leadership.

Strategies for Preserving the Faith of Our Fathers

Education and Catechism

Education and catechesis are important strategies for preserving the Catholic tradition. The Church must make her members, especially the young, aware of the rich faith. This can be done through technical and religious education in schools or through informal activities such as religious instruction at home and in the community. By teaching the traditions of the Church, Catholics can deepen their understanding of their heritage and be inspired to pass it on to future generations (Catechesi Tradendae, 1979, p. 55).

Integrating Tradition into Public Life

Integrating tradition into public life is another important strategy for preserving Catholic tradition. This can be done through liturgical celebrations, worship, and other cultural activities that reflect the Church's rich heritage. By integrating tradition into the fabric of public life, Catholics can realise the richness of their faith and the possibility of passing it on to future generations (Sacrosanctum Concilium, 1963, p. 40).

Interaction with Modern Society

Interaction with modern society is also important for the preservation of the Catholic tradition. In today's digital age, churches need to use technology and other means to share their traditions and values with the wider world. This can be done through social media, websites, and other online platforms that reach a broad audience. Through her close relationship with people today, the Church can ensure that her traditions remain valid and wise for people of all ages and backgrounds (Pope Francis, Evangelical Joy, 2013, p. 47).

Promoting Tradition

Finally, promoting tradition in the Church is key to preserving Catholic tradition. This includes creating an environment that celebrates and supports religious leadership. This can be done by encouraging cultural practices such as fasting, prayer, and feasting and by promoting education and understanding of the Church's rich history and traditions. By supporting traditions, the Church can ensure that these traditions remain in the hearts of believers.

Preserving the Catholic tradition requires a multifaceted approach. It's about finding the right balance between preserving the past and participating in the present. By using the strategies outlined above, the Church can ensure that her traditions are preserved for future generations. Similarly, defending the Catholic tradition is more than defending historical practice. This is to preserve the essence of the faith and the Church herself. In the face of today's problems, such as secularism, globalisation, and progress, the Church must cooperate in the preservation of tradition.

Addressing the Misconceptions of Miracles

Misconceptions about miracles are common, often stemming from misunderstandings or misinterpretations of biblical teachings and theological concepts. This misunderstanding often arises from a misunderstanding of the purpose of miracles and their role in faith. Many people believe that miracles are limited to Biblical times (historical events) and are not valid or possible in the modern world as they have nothing to do with today's life; others think that miracles cannot be explained.

However, the Catholic Church says that miracles are not limited to the past, nor are they events of divine intervention, but can and do occur in all ages as a sign of God's presence, love and power in the world (Catechism of the Catholic Church, 2003, p. 156).

Biblical and Theological Foundations

Belief in the continued existence of miracles is based on Scriptures and theological thought. Throughout the Bible, from the Old Testament to the New Testament, we find cases of miracles that show that God has the ability to mobilise world culture. These miracles are signs of God's presence and power, demonstrating the truthfulness of the Gospel (John 2:1-11; John 11:1-44).

The Role of Miracles in the Church Today

In the Catholic tradition, miracles are understood as events that come into this world from the Kingdom of God. They help strengthen believers' faith, inspire awe and wonder, and point to the reality of God's presence among us. Miracles are not just historical events; they are evidence of God's constant work in the world.

In order to eliminate the misconception that 'miracles are a thing of the past', it is important to emphasise their importance and reality in the life of faith. This can be done through education, catechism, and personal testimony. By sharing the stories of today's miracles and the Church's teachings on these subjects, we can help dispel the idea that miracles only occurred in ancient times. The idea that miracles are a thing of the past is a mistake that ignores the fact that God is still performing miracles in a world of panic.

FAQ and Troubleshooting

People often question the reality of miracles or find plausible explanations for miraculous events. The Church recognises the need for wisdom and thoughtfulness but also emphasises the importance of knowing God's hand in emergencies (Dei Verbum, 1965, p. 51). The purpose of science is not to replace it but to complement it and provide a deeper understanding of the beliefs and mysteries of the natural world.

The Catholic Church's perspective on miracles shows the relationship between faith and reason. Miracles are not seen as a violation of the laws of science but as a manifestation of God's power and presence in the world. The supernatural and the natural are both God's plan. By accepting miracles, we can strengthen our faith and our relationship with God because they are important signs of God's love and care for us.

Miracles do not violate the laws of nature or the effectiveness of magic; they also demonstrate God's extraordinary power and willingness to intervene in our lives. They are a testament to His sovereignty and His desire to bring goodness to the world, even in the midst of difficulties and troubles.

Dispelling misconceptions about miracles is important to helping people see miracles for what they really are. Miracles are not meant to deceive or confuse but to inspire fear and wonder at God's works.

Finally, miracles are an invitation to faith and a relationship with God. They ask us to trust in His help and open our hearts to His grace. When we accept the truth of these miracles, our lives undergo a great change, and we come closer to God and His blessings.

CHAPTER VII

Call for Collaboration and Solidarity

Collaboration and solidarity are vital to the prosperity of the Catholic Church in Nigeria. When we work together and support one another, we can build a more vibrant Church. This unity is rooted in our common faith and mission. By embracing diversity and encouraging inclusion, we can create harmonious and effective communities. Our collective efforts can accomplish much more than individual efforts. Through cooperation and solidarity, we can build a bright future for the Church in Nigeria.

Building Support Networks Among Priests and Religious

Priests and religious in Nigeria face various challenges in their ministry. These challenges include isolation, burnout, and spiritual dryness. To address these challenges, building support networks among Priests is essential. There is great significance in collaborating and forming solidarity among clergy and religious. Scripture provides a strong foundation for the concept of support networks among believers. Ecclesiastes 4:9–10 highlights this clearly, and it states, "*Two are better than one; because they have a good return for their labour. If either of them falls down, one can help the other up."* This clearly illustrates the value of companionship and mutual assistance. It acknowledges that life is full of challenges and that having a support system in place can make those challenges more manageable. By working together, individuals can achieve more and overcome obstacles that would be difficult to face alone. In the same vein, Jesus's relationship with His disciples demonstrates His value for collaboration. Throughout the Gospel, we see Jesus forming a close community with His disciples, teaching and guiding them and providing emotional and spiritual support. In John 15:12-13, Jesus says, *"This is my commandment: Love one another just as I have loved you. "There is no greater love than giving one's life for one's friends."* This shows the depth of love and support that must exist within the Christian community.

Early Christian communities also represent models of support networks. In Acts 2:42-47, we read about the early believers devoting themselves to fellowship, breaking bread together, and sharing what they had with those in need. This shows a strong sense of community and mutual support among early Christians. This biblical example has important implications for modern faith communities. It reminds us of the importance of community and support in our spiritual journey. Just as Jesus and His disciples helped each other, we are called to help one another in our faith. By building a strong support network within our faith community, we can strengthen our faith, overcome challenges, and grow together in our walk with God.

Benefits of a Support Network

Support networks between clergy and religious people provide many benefits, including emotional support, spiritual growth, and practical help. Sharing experiences and problems with others who understand the demands of ministry can help prevent burnout and isolation (Lumen Gentium, 1964, p. 50). Support networks can also provide opportunities for spiritual growth through communal prayer, meditation, and discernment (Presbyterorum Ordinis, 1967, p. 18).

Emotional support: Every Priest needs emotional support as they often face significant stress and challenges in their ministry. These challenges can lead to feelings of isolation and burnout. Having a support network allows Priests and religious to share their experiences and feelings with others who understand their unique situations. This sharing can be incredibly therapeutic, offering relief and comfort. For example, when a Priest feels overwhelmed by the demands of his parish, having a trusted group of fellow Priests to confide in can provide the necessary emotional support to help him cope. In Galatians 6:2, Paul writes, *"Bear one another's burdens, and thus fulfil the law of Christ.*" This passage emphasises the obligation of Christians to support one another emotionally to help bear the burdens of life's trials. By doing so, Priests and religious leaders will know that they are not alone in their struggles and can gain strength and encouragement from a support network.

Spiritual growth: A support network is also essential for spiritual growth. It provides opportunities for communal prayer, reflection and discernment, which are essential for deepening one's faith. When Priests and religious come together to pray and reflect on their experiences, new insights and a deeper understanding of their spiritual journey are gained. This is reinforced in Matthew 18:20, where Jesus says, "*For where two or three gather in my name, there am I with them.*" This connection is essential for maintaining a strong spiritual life, especially in the face of the demands and challenges of ministry.

Support networks can also provide opportunities for spiritual direction and mentorship, where more experienced Priests and religious can guide and support those who are newer to the ministry. This mentorship can be invaluable, helping to nurture and develop the spiritual lives of those involved.

Practical Help: In addition to emotional and spiritual support, support networks can offer practical help. This can include sharing resources, offering advice on ministry-related issues, and providing assistance in times of need. For example, suppose a Priest is struggling with a particular aspect of his ministry, such as managing a difficult parish situation. In that case, he can turn to his support network for practical advice and guidance.

Support networks can also facilitate the sharing of resources, such as liturgical materials, educational resources, and pastoral programs. By pooling their resources and knowledge, Priests and religious can better serve their communities and enhance their ministry. This practical support is grounded in the Christian principle of mutual aid, as seen in Acts 2:44-45, where the early Christians '*had everything in common*' and '*sold property and possessions to give to anyone who had need*'.

In his apostolic exhortation, *Pastores Dabo Vobis*, Pope John Paul II emphasised the importance of fraternity among Priests, noting that it helps prevent the isolation that can lead to burnout (John Paul II, 1992, p. 74). By fostering strong support networks, the Church can help ensure that her Priests and religious remain healthy and effective in their ministry.

The importance of support networks is deeply rooted in both the Bible and Catholic teaching. As previously mentioned, Ecclesiastes 4:9-10 underscores the value of companionship and mutual support. Similarly, in 1 Corinthians 12:12-27, Paul uses the metaphor of the body to describe the Church, emphasising that all members are interconnected and must support one another. This passage highlights the theological foundation for support networks, illustrating that just as the body needs all its parts to function effectively, so too does the Church need all her members to support one another.

Official Church documents also reinforce the importance of support networks. *Lumen Gentium (1964)* and *Presbyterorum Ordinis* (1967) both emphasise the communal nature of the Church and the need for mutual support among her members. These documents highlight the Church's commitment to fostering strong support networks among Priests and religious, recognising their essential role in promoting emotional, spiritual, and practical well-being.

Strategy for Building a Support Network

Building a support network between clergy and religious people requires dedicated effort and commitment. Regular meetings, such as monthly meetings or annual retreats, can provide opportunities for exchange, prayer, and fellowship (Presbyterorum Ordinis, 1967, p. 18). Technologies such as social media groups and online forums can also facilitate connections and support between clergy and religious leaders (Pope Francis, 2014).

Meetings

One effective strategy for building a support network is to organise regular meetings. This may take the form of monthly meetings where Priests and religious come together to discuss their experiences, share problems, and support each other. These meetings may include structured activities such as group prayer, Scripture study, and discussion of current issues facing the Church. The main goal is to create a space where Priests and religious leaders feel understood and supported by their peers. *Presbyterorum Ordinis* (1967) emphasises the importance of this social activity, stating that regular interaction between clergy promotes unity and mutual support (p. 18).

Retreats

Annual retreats are another powerful tool for building support networks. These retreats offer a longer period for reflection, rest, and rejuvenation away from the daily pressures of ministry. They can provide a setting for deeper spiritual growth through extended periods of prayer, silence, and guided reflections. The benefits of these retreats are profound, as they allow Priests and religious to reconnect with their vocation and with each other in a meaningful way. During these retreats, they can experience the presence of Christ in a communal setting, echoing the words of Jesus in Matthew 18:20, *"For where two or three gather in my name, there am I with them."*

Use of Technology

In the modern era, technology plays a crucial role in maintaining and building support networks. Social media groups, online forums, and messaging apps can help clergy and religious people stay connected despite geographic distance. These platforms provide a space for instant communication, sharing resources, and providing immediate support. Pope Francis has often encouraged the use of technology to strengthen bonds within the Church. In his message for the 48th World Communications Day, the Pope said, "The revolution taking place in the field of communications and information technology is a great and exciting challenge" (Pope Francis, 2014).

This continuous line of communication ensures that support is always available, making it easier for individuals to reach out when they need help. Furthermore, these platforms can host virtual meetings and prayer sessions, allowing clergy who are unable to attend physical gatherings to participate and benefit from communal support.

Mentorship Programs

Establishing mentorship programs within dioceses can also significantly enhance support networks. Pairing experienced Priests with those who are newly ordained or facing specific challenges can provide personalised guidance and support. Mentors can share their wisdom, offer advice, and provide a listening ear, helping to overcome the challenges of priestly life. In Pastores Dabo Vobis, Pope John Paul II emphasised the importance of mentoring, saying that young Priests should be accompanied and supported by older and more experienced colleagues (John Paul II, 1992, p. 60).

Mentoring programs can also help foster a sense of continuity and tradition within a church. By building relationships between different generations of clergy, the program ensures the transfer of valuable knowledge and experience and enriches the entire community. Biblical principles of discipleship further emphasise the importance of such mentoring relationships, as seen in the relationship between Paul and Timothy (2 Timothy 2:2).

Joint Project

Participating in joint projects strengthens the support network as it provides shared goals and fosters teamwork. Clergy and religious leaders may work together on community service programs, social justice initiatives, or parish development projects. These collaborative efforts not only benefit the broader community but also strengthen the bonds between participants. Working together on such projects gives them a sense of purpose and accomplishment and reinforces the feeling that they are part of a larger mission.

The concept of teamwork is deeply rooted in the New Testament. In 1 Corinthians 12:12-27, Paul describes the Church as a body with many parts, each contributing to the whole. This metaphor highlights the importance of collaboration and mutual support, illustrating that the success of the Church depends on the combined efforts of all her members.

Creating Safe Spaces

Another crucial strategy is creating safe spaces where Priests and religious can express their concerns and challenges without fear of judgment. These safe spaces can be physical, such as designated rooms in parish centres, or conceptual, such as support groups that prioritise confidentiality and empathy. The creation of such spaces encourages open communication and vulnerability, which are essential for building trust and support. Hebrews 10:24-25 says, "*And let us consider how we may spur one another on towards love and good deeds, not giving up meeting together, as some are in the habit of doing, but encouraging one another.*" This passage highlights the need for continual support and encouragement within the Christian community.

In summary, building support networks among Priests and religious requires intentional strategies that foster regular interaction. By implementing these strategies outlined, the Church can ensure that her clergy and religious are well-supported and able to fulfil their vocations effectively.

Fostering Unity Within the Church Community

Unity within the church community is essential for her growth and effectiveness in carrying out her mission. The Bible emphasises the importance of unity among believers, emphasising that it is both a reflection of God's nature and a witness to the world. In John 17:21, Jesus prays, *"Father, may they all be one, just as you are in me and I am in You. May they also be among Us so that the world may believe that You sent me."* This prayer emphasises the sacred desire for unity among the faithful, which should be the guiding principle of the Church.

Several key strategies can be implemented to promote unity within the church community, and they are:

Promote inclusive participation

Inclusion is the basis of harmony. The Church must ensure that all members, regardless of background, feel respected and included. This includes actively encouraging participation in Church activities among people of various ages, ethnic groups, and social classes. Inclusion can be promoted through diverse worship styles, inclusive language, and targeted outreach. By recognising and celebrating the unique gifts and contributions of each member, Churches can build stronger, more cohesive communities.

St. Paul in 1st Corinthians 12:12-27 provides a clear biblical basis for inclusion. Paul describes the Church as a body made up of several parts, each of which is necessary to perform her function. He wrote, *"For just as the body is one and has many parts, and the members of the body, though many, are one body, so also is Christ"* (1 Corinthians 12:12). This metaphor emphasises that each member plays an important role and that unity is achieved through diversity.

Promote open communication

Effective communication is critical to fostering unity. Churches must create an environment where open and honest dialogue is encouraged. This can be achieved through regular meetings, discussion groups and forums where participants can express their opinions and concerns. Leaders must model active listening and demonstrate a willingness to resolve problems constructively. Ephesians 4:15-16 highlights the importance of communication in building up the Church. *"Instead, speaking the truth in love, we will grow to become in every respect the mature body of Him who is the head, that is, Christ. From Him, the whole body joined and held together by every supporting ligament, grows and builds itself up in love, as each part does its work.*" By fostering a culture of open communication, the Church can address conflicts and misunderstandings, paving the way for greater unity.

Encourage collaborative worship

Worship is a central activity in the life of the Church and a powerful tool for fostering unity. Collaborative worship involves incorporating different styles and traditions to reflect the diversity of the congregation. This can include a mix of contemporary and traditional music, multilingual services, and incorporating various cultural expressions of faith. This allows the Church to respect the diversity of her members and create a more inclusive worship experience. Psalm 132:1 perfectly captures the essence of unity in worship. *"How good and how beautiful it is for God's people to live together in unity!"* When the Church gathers for worship, it becomes a visible expression of the unity for which Christ prayed in John 17. Worshipping together not only enhances the worship experience but also strengthens the bonds between members.

Provide collaborative service opportunities

Service is a practical expression of faith and a powerful means of strengthening unity. Churches can organise collaborative service projects that bring together members from diverse backgrounds to achieve a common goal. Whether it's community service activities, social justice initiatives or mission trips, these events provide members with opportunities to build relationships and experience the joy of serving together. In Galatians 6:2, Paul exhorts believers to *"bear one another's burdens, and thus fulfil the law of Christ.*" Through joint service projects, churches can put this commandment into practice by fostering solidarity and mutual support. As members serve together, they witness firsthand the results of their joint efforts and strengthen their unity and commitment to the Church's mission.

Overcoming Obstacles on the Path to Integration

Despite the Church's efforts to promote unity, obstacles often arise that need to be removed. This may include cultural, generational, or theological differences. Churches must actively identify and remove these obstacles to create more unified communities. One effective approach is education and dialogue. Providing members with opportunities to learn about different cultures and perspectives can help bridge gaps and promote mutual understanding. Additionally, theological education that emphasises the core tenets of the faith and the importance of unity can help mitigate doctrinal divisions.

Philippians 2:2-4 provides guidance on overcoming barriers to unity, *"Then make my joy complete by being like-minded, having the same love, being one in spirit and of one mind. Do nothing out of selfish ambition or vain conceit. Rather, in humility, value others above yourselves, not looking to your own interests but each of you to the interests of the others.*" By fostering a spirit of humility and mutual respect, the Church can overcome barriers and work towards greater unity.

Role of Church Leadership in Promoting Unity

Church leaders play a crucial role in fostering unity within the community. They must model the principles of inclusivity, open communication, collaborative worship, and joint service. Leaders should be approachable, actively engage with all members, and work to create an environment where everyone feels valued and included. Leaders are exhorted in 1 Peter 5:2-3, *"Be shepherds of God's flock that is under your care, watching over them—not because you must, but because you are willing, as God wants you to be; not pursuing dishonest gain, but eager to serve; not lording it over those entrusted to you, but being examples to the flock.*" By embodying these qualities, church leaders can effectively guide their communities towards greater unity.

Official Church Documents on Unity

The importance of unity within the Church is also emphasised in official Church documents. *Lumen Gentium,* one of the principal documents of the Second Vatican Council, highlights the Church as the people of God called to unity in faith and love. "The Church in Christ has the essence of the Eucharist. That is, it is a sign and an instrument of communion with God and the unity of all people" (Lumen Gentium, 1964, p. 1). Likewise, *Nostra Aetate* emphasises the importance of dialogue and understanding between different religious communities as a path towards unity and peace. It encourages respect and cooperation and says, "The Church, therefore, calls upon her children to recognise, preserve and promote what is good in their witness to the Christian faith and life, with prudence and love, through dialogue and cooperation with believers of other religions" (Nostra Aetate, 1965, p. 2).

Moreover, in his encyclical *Evangelii Gaudium*, Pope Francis emphasised the need for unity within the Church and the wider community. He wrote, "The Church must guide everyone – priests, religious and laity – in this art of accompaniment, this art teaches us to take off our shoes before someone else's sacred ground" (Joy of the Gospel, 2013, p. 169).

Building the Laity for Effective Collaboration in the Parish

Effective cooperation between clergy and laity is vital to the vitality and mission of the Church. The Second Vatican Council emphasised the active role of the laity in the mission of the Church, recognising that all baptized members participate in the priesthood of Christ and are called to contribute to the life and mission of the Church (Lumen Gentium, 1964, page 10). Preparing lay people to collaborate effectively includes education, empowerment, and developing a culture of cooperation and mutual respect within the parish.

Understanding the Role of the Laity

The lay faithful are not mere bystanders to the mission of the Church. They are active participants. According *to Lumen Gentium*, "The laity pursue the Kingdom of God by their vocation, attending to worldly affairs and managing them according to God's plan" (1964, p. 31). This means that lay people are called to bring their faith into all aspects of their lives, to influence the world around them and to contribute to the mission of the Church. The Catechism of the Catholic Church states, "The laity, as their vocation, pursue the kingdom of God, engage in worldly affairs and deal with them according to the will of God" (CCC 898). This involvement requires a deep understanding of the faith, a strong spiritual foundation, and a commitment to living the Gospel in daily life.

Education and Training

A key step in preparing laypeople to collaborate effectively is providing them with the necessary training and education. This includes catechesis, theological education, and practical training in various ministries. Education should cover the basics of the Catholic faith, the Bible, Church teachings, and the sacraments. It must also address contemporary problems and how to apply Catholic principles to those problems. The Church's literature provides many resources for such teaching. For example, *Christifideles Laici* emphasised the importance of the formation of the laity, saying, "The laity must be formed so that their Christian consciousness can perform its special function in society" (1988, p. 59).

Empowerment and Encouragement

Empowering the laity means recognising their gifts and talents and encouraging them to participate actively in parish life. This can be achieved by providing opportunities for laypeople to lead and serve in a variety of ministries, including liturgical functions, catechesis, outreach programs, and administrative duties. Encouragement from parish leadership is essential to helping lay people feel valued and motivated to contribute. Apostle Paul emphasises the importance of recognising and using various gifts within the Church. In 1 Corinthians 12:4-7, he wrote: "*There are different gifts, but the same Spirit imparts them. The service is different, but the Lord is the same. There are different things, but the same God works in all things and in all people.*" By recognising and nurturing these gifts, parishes can become more vibrant and dynamic.

Collaborative Culture

Building a culture of collaboration in a parish requires intentional effort from both clergy and laity. The clergy must be accessible and open to the participation of the laity, creating an atmosphere of trust and mutual respect. The laity, on the other hand, must see themselves as partners in the Church's mission and be willing to accept responsibility. Regular communication and transparent decision-making processes are essential for collaboration. Parish councils, committees and advisory councils can provide a platform for lay participation in parish management and planning. This structure ensures that the public's voice is reflected in the decision-making process.

In *The Joy of the Gospel*, Pope Francis emphasised the need for a united Church and declared, "The Church that goes forward is a community of missionary disciples who take the first steps, participate and support, bear fruit and rejoice" (2013, p. 24). This vision calls for the creation of a Church in which all members, clergy and laity, work together in a spirit of unity and common mission.

Practical Steps to Foster Collaboration

To build effective collaboration, parishes can take several practical steps:

Lay Leadership Training: Offer leadership training programs to help lay people develop the skills and confidence they need to lead parish initiatives. This may include workshops on public speaking, project management, and conflict resolution.

Mentoring Program: Create a mentoring program where experienced lay and clergy leaders can guide and support new members. Mentoring helps foster personal growth and build a strong foundation for future leaders.

Inclusive planning process: Involve the laity in planning and implementing parish activities. Solicit feedback through surveys, town halls, and focus groups to ensure diverse perspectives are included.

Mechanisms for regular feedback: Create opportunities for laypeople to provide regular feedback to parish leaders. This can be done through suggestion boxes, feedback forms, and regular review meetings.

Recognise Contributions: Publicly recognise and celebrate the contributions of lay members. This recognition may come in the form of an award, certificate, or special mention at a parish event.

The biblical and theological foundations of lay participation are deeply rooted in Scripture and Church tradition. The Second Vatican Council document *Apostolicam Actuositatem* emphasises the active role of the laity, "The laity derive their apostolic rights and responsibilities from their union with Christ, their Head. Through Baptism, they are united to the Mystical Body of Christ, and through Confirmation, they are strengthened by the power of the Holy Spirit, to whom the Lord Himself bestows an apostolate" (1965, p. 3).

Also, the life of the early Church provides numerous examples of laypeople participating in ministry. In Acts 6:1-7, the apostles emphasised the importance of lay ministry in the early Christian community when they appointed seven deacons to help distribute food. This delegation of responsibility allowed the apostles to focus on prayer and ministry of the word and demonstrated a collaborative approach to ministry.

Challenges in Building Collaborations

Building effective collaboration with the laity offers many opportunities but also challenges. Resistance to change, lack of resources, and potential conflict can hinder progress. However, these problems can be addressed through ongoing education, open dialogue, and commitment to the Church's mission.

One major concern is the possibility of clericalism, where clergy may be reluctant to share responsibilities with the laity. Overcoming this requires a shift in mindset, recognising that collaboration enhances the Church's mission rather than diminishes clerical authority. Another challenge is ensuring that all lay members, regardless of their background or level of education, feel included and valued. This can be addressed by providing accessible and inclusive formation programs and creating a welcoming parish environment.

Collaborative efforts between clergy and laity based on biblical and theological principles can lead to a more vibrant, dynamic, and inclusive church community. As the Church continues to navigate the complexities of modern society, fostering effective collaboration will be critical to her growth and witness. The vision of a united Church with clergy and laity working together in unity is not only achievable but necessary to fulfill the mission of the Church. By developing the laity to collaborate effectively, the Church can become a powerful force for good, embodying God's love and grace in the world.

Partnering With Other Christian Denominations

Partnering with other Christian denominations is an essential aspect of fostering unity and promoting the mission of the Church in contemporary society. In Nigeria, where religious diversity is a hallmark, collaboration among Christian denominations can significantly enhance the Church's impact.

The call for unity among Christians is deeply rooted in Scripture. Jesus' prayer for unity in John 17:21 is a profound expression of His desire for His followers to be one. *"That they all may be one, as You, Father, are in Me, and I in You; that they also may be one in Us, that the world may believe that You sent Me."* This prayer underscores the importance of unity as a testament to the world of the truth of the Gospel.

Apostle Paul also emphasised the importance of unity in his letters. In Ephesians 4:3-6, Paul urges, *"Make every effort to keep the unity of the Spirit through the bond of peace. There is one body and one Spirit, just as you were called to one hope when you were called; one Lord, one faith, one Baptism; one God and Father of all, who is over all and through all and in all."* This passage highlights the theological basis for unity, emphasising that all believers share the same foundational elements of faith.

The Catholic Church has long recognised the importance of ecumenism, or promoting unity among Christian denominations. The Second Vatican Council's Decree "Unitatis Redintegratio" states, "The restoration of unity among all Christians is one of the main tasks of the Second Vatican Council. The Lord Christ established one Church and one Church only. However, many Christian communities present their people as the true heirs of Jesus Christ. All of them actually claim to follow the Lord, but they think differently and take different paths as if Christ Himself were divided" (Unitatis Redintegratio, 1964, p. One).

Additionally, the Catechism of the Catholic Church reaffirms the Church's commitment to ecumenism by emphasising common Baptism and common faith among Christians. "Baptism is the basis of communion between all Christians, including those who are not yet in full communion with the Catholic Church" (Catechism of the Catholic Church, no. 1271). This foundation provides the basis for dialogue and cooperation between the various Christian denominations.

A Practical Approach to Ecumenical Partnerships

Building effective partnerships with other Christian denominations requires focused effort and practical action. One key approach is dialogue and mutual understanding. Organising joint meetings, forums, and discussion groups can help us better understand each other's traditions, beliefs, and customs. This dialogue must be based on a sincere desire for respect and unity.

Another practical approach is shared ministry and service projects. Partnerships in community service initiatives such as feeding the hungry, providing health care, and supporting education can demonstrate the power of Christian unity in addressing social needs. This joint effort not only meets a practical need but also serves as a testament to the transforming power of the Gospel.

Joint worship and prayer meetings are also effective ways to strengthen unity. These events provide an opportunity for Christians of various faiths to come together to worship, share prayers, and celebrate their common faith. Such gatherings can strengthen relationships and promote solidarity among believers.

Benefits of Ecumenical Partnership

Partnerships with other Christian denominations offer numerous benefits to the Church and society as a whole. One important benefit is that your testimony of the Gospel is strengthened. When Christians from diverse traditions come together, they provide powerful testimony of the unifying power of the Gospel that can attract non-believers and strengthen the faith of current believers.

Ecumenical partnerships also provide opportunities for shared learning and growth. Diverse faiths bring unique perspectives and strengths that can enrich the faith and practice of all participants. For example, one sect may have a strong tradition of social justice, while another may excel at liturgical worship. By learning from one another, Churches can improve their ministries and better serve their communities.

Ecumenical partnerships can promote peace and reconciliation. In areas where religious tensions are high, showing unity between Christian faiths can help reduce conflict and spread a message of peace. This unity can serve as a model for broader social reconciliation and cooperation.

The Troubles and Remedies for Ecumenical Partnerships

The benefits of ecumenical partnerships are significant, but there are also challenges. One common problem is doctrinal differences. Different faiths have different beliefs and practices, which can be an obstacle to unity. It is important to approach these differences humbly and be willing to listen and learn from one another. Focusing on commonalities and shared beliefs can help alleviate these problems.

Another problem is historical tension and distrust. In some cases, historical conflicts and misunderstandings have led to deep divisions between faiths. Solving these problems requires a commitment to forgiveness and reconciliation and building new relationships based on trust and respect. Engaging in honest and open conversations about past hurts can pave the way for healing and new unity.

Practical considerations such as coordination of joint activities and resource management may also be problematic. Effective planning, clear communication, and a collaborative spirit are essential to overcoming these logistical obstacles. Forming a joint committee or task force can help address these practicalities and ensure that joint efforts proceed smoothly.

The early Church provides a model of ecumenical unity that can guide modern efforts. In the book of Acts, we see a united community of diverse believers from different backgrounds. Acts 2:42-47 describes how the early Christians devoted themselves to the apostles' teaching, to the fellowship, to the breaking of bread, and to prayer. All believers were together and shared everything. This highlights several key elements of unity: common teaching, fellowship, worship, and mutual support. These elements are essential for building and maintaining unity among Christian denominations today. Following the example of the early Church, modern Christians can strive for a more unified and effective witness.

Ecumenical Initiatives in Nigeria

In Nigeria, several ecumenical initiatives have demonstrated the potential for unity among Christian denominations. For example, the Christian Association of Nigeria (CAN) is a prominent ecumenical organisation that brings together various Christian denominations to promote unity and address common concerns. CAN has played a crucial role in advocating for religious freedom, social justice, and peace in Nigeria.

Local initiatives, such as joint prayer meetings, inter-denominational worship services, and collaborative social projects, have also shown the benefits of ecumenical partnerships. These initiatives provide practical examples of how Christians from different traditions can work together to advance the mission of the Church and address the needs of their communities.

Partnering with other Christian denominations is not just an option but a necessity for the Church in Nigeria. The theological foundations for unity are clear, and the benefits of ecumenical partnerships are profound. By engaging in intentional dialogue, collaborative ministry, and shared worship, Christian denominations can strengthen their witness, enrich their faith, and promote peace and reconciliation.

As Christians in Nigeria and around the world seek to live out Jesus' prayer for unity, they can draw inspiration from Scripture, official Church documents, and practical examples of successful partnerships. By embracing the call to unity, the Church can more effectively fulfil her mission and bring the light of the Gospel to a world in need.

CHAPTER VIII

The Future of the Catholic Faith in Nigeria

As someone deeply connected to the Catholic community in Nigeria, I am inspired by the resilience and vibrancy of the faithful. The Church's ability to adapt to changing times while remaining steadfast in her core mission is a testament to her enduring strength. I have witnessed firsthand how digital platforms have brought the faith to life in new ways, particularly among the youth who are eager to engage with their faith on a deeper level. The Church's commitment to social justice and advocacy continues to be a beacon of hope in challenging times. I am optimistic that the Catholic Church in Nigeria will continue to thrive, embracing new opportunities while remaining true to her foundational principles.

The future of the Catholic faith in Nigeria is shaped by a complex interplay of demographic, technological, socio-political, and cultural factors. By leveraging the opportunities presented by these changes and addressing the associated challenges, the Catholic Church can continue to grow and have a profound impact on Nigerian society.

The future of the Catholic faith in Nigeria is a topic of great importance and interest. As the Church continues to grow and evolve in Nigeria, she faces a number of challenges and opportunities. Addressing these challenges and embracing these opportunities are sure ways for the Catholic Church in Nigeria to thrive and be a source of hope and inspiration for all Nigerians.

Trends and Predictions

We live in an ever-changing environment; trends and predictions change, and they are bound to affect every aspect of life, especially one's spiritual life. Understanding and responding to these key trends, combined with the Church's ability to navigate through a changing environment while remaining true to her core mission, is inspiring, and it can help chart a course that ensures her continued relevance and influence.

As someone deeply connected to the Nigerian Catholic community, I see immense potential for growth and positive impact. The youth's enthusiasm, the embrace of digital platforms, and the commitment to social justice all signal a vibrant future for the Church. The challenge will be to harness these trends effectively, ensuring that the Church remains a beacon of hope and a force for good in Nigeria.

As we look to the future of the Catholic faith in Nigeria, it's essential to consider the trends and predictions that will shape the Church's trajectory.

Growth in the Population of the Nigerian Catholic Church

The Nigerian Catholic Church is poised for continued growth, driven by the country's population boom and the Church's missionary zeal. This growth is not just in numbers but also in the depth of faith and commitment among the faithful. As Jesus commissioned His disciples to go and make disciples of all nations (Matthew 28:19), the Church in Nigeria takes this mandate seriously, actively engaging in evangelization and outreach. Nigeria's population is rapidly increasing, with significant urban migration. By 2050, Nigeria is expected to become the third most populous country globally, with a substantial portion of her population living in urban areas. Consequently, it is predictable that the Church will need to expand her urban ministries, focusing on addressing the spiritual and social needs of city dwellers. This may involve establishing more parishes in urban centres, offering social services, and creating community support networks to cater to the challenges of urban life.

Invariably, as the Catholic Church in Nigeria grows, the demand for Priests also increases. The Church must invest in strong Priest formation programs to ensure that new Priests are well-prepared to serve their communities. This includes pastoral and leadership skills as well as theological training. John (20:21) reminds us that just as the Father sent Jesus, so too does Jesus send us. This emphasises the importance of preparing Priests to be effective ministers of the Gospel in a rapidly changing society.

There will also be an increased demand for catechesis and social services. Catechesis is essential in fostering the faith of both new and existing members and ensuring that they are firmly rooted in the teachings of the Church, as well as the Church's commitment to social justice and the poor. Matthew 25:31-46 calls for providing social services to the most vulnerable in society. This includes education, healthcare and helping those in need.

Meeting these needs requires a creative response from church leaders. This may include innovative approaches to clergy formation, such as online or distance learning programs. Partnerships with other organisations within and outside the Church may be necessary to deliver social services more effectively. Church leaders must be forward-thinking and proactive, anticipating future needs and adapting accordingly.

Secularization and Religious Pluralism

Secularization refers to the process by which religious institutions, practices, and beliefs lose their social significance. This trend is often accompanied by the rise of secular ideologies and the relegation of religion to the private sphere. In Nigeria, the influence of secularization can be seen in various aspects of society, including politics, education, and daily life.

As Nigerian society becomes more secular, the influence of religious institutions on public life decreases noticeably. This shift challenges the Catholic Church's traditional role in shaping societal values and norms. The Church must find ways to remain relevant in a context where secular ideologies increasingly dominate public discourse.

Younger generations in Nigeria are exhibiting more liberal attitudes towards religion. Many are questioning traditional beliefs and practices, leading to a more individualised approach to spirituality. This trend offers the Church an opportunity to engage with young people in innovative ways, fostering a faith that is both personal and communal. Therefore, the Church must engage more robustly with Nigerian culture and other faith traditions to remain relevant and effective in her mission.

Religious pluralism refers to the coexistence of various religious beliefs in a society. Nigeria is a country with high religious diversity, with Christianity, Islam, and Traditional African religions being the main religions. This religious diversity presents both opportunities and challenges for the Catholic Church. On the one hand, it provides an opportunity for interreligious dialogue and cooperation, promoted by the declaration of the Second Vatican Council Nostra Aetate (1965). On the other hand, it requires the Church to traverse the complexities of religious pluralism while remaining faithful to her own teachings.

To effectively engage with secularization and religious pluralism, the Catholic Church in Nigeria must embrace Nigerian culture. This means contextualizing her message in a way that resonates with the cultural values and norms of the Nigerian people. It also means actively participating in cultural activities and events, demonstrating that the Church is not separate from Nigerian society but an integral part of it.

The Catholic Church in Nigeria must be proactive in addressing the challenges posed by secularization and religious pluralism, engage more robustly with Nigerian culture and other faith traditions, and embrace inter-religious dialogue and collaboration.

Technology and Catholic Communication in Nigeria

Technology is rapidly changing the way we communicate and interact with the world, and the Catholic Church in Nigeria is not immune to these changes. As stated in *Evangelii Gaudium* (2013), the Church must embrace technology as a tool for evangelization and community building. By harnessing digital platforms, the Church can reach new generations and promote the Gospel in innovative ways. Technology has revolutionised communication, making it easier and faster to connect with people around the world. In Nigeria, where internet penetration is increasing rapidly, the Church can use digital platforms such as social media, websites, and mobile apps to reach a wider audience. These platforms allow the Church to share messages, videos, and other content with people who may not have access to traditional forms of communication.

Evangelization is at the core of the Church's mission, and technology can greatly enhance these efforts. Through digital platforms, the Church can reach people who may be hesitant to attend traditional Church services or who may be searching for spiritual guidance online. By providing engaging and informative content, the Church can draw people closer to the Gospel and invite them to deepen their faith. Technology also allows the Church to build online communities where people can connect, share their faith, and support one another. These communities can take many forms, from social media groups to online forums and chat rooms. By fostering a sense of belonging and connection among members, churches can create a positive environment where people feel valued and cared for.

Digital platforms also provide the Church with the ease to address pressing social issues like poverty, inequality, and political instability, drawing on Catholic Social Teaching and the preferential option for the poor (Gaudium et Spes, 1965; Evangelii Gaudium, 2013).

Technology has the potential to revolutionize Catholic communication, evangelization, and community building in Nigeria. As the world becomes increasingly digital, the Church must adapt to these changes. This means embracing new technologies and finding creative ways to use them for good. In doing so, the Church can continue to spread the message of God's love and mercy throughout Nigeria and beyond.

The Nigerian Catholic Church: Promoting National Unity, Peace, And Development

For many years, the Nigerian Catholic Church has served as both a stronghold and a source of hope for the nation. As Matthew 28:18-20 reminds us, the Church has a vital role to play in promoting national unity, peace, and development. In the face of challenges and opportunities, the Church must continue to be a force for good, proclaiming the Gospel and serving the Nigerian people with hope and joy.

One of the key roles of the Nigerian Catholic Church is to promote national unity. Through her teachings and actions, the Church promotes the values of tolerance, respect, and unity that are essential for building a strong and united nation.

Peace is another core principle of the Catholic faith, and the Nigerian Church is committed to promoting peace at all levels of society. This includes advocating for peace in conflict zones, promoting dialogue and reconciliation between conflict parties, and working to address the root causes of violence. By promoting a culture of peace, the Church contributes to the overall stability and development of Nigeria.

Development is not only about economic growth; it is also about human flourishing and the common good. The Catholic Church in Nigeria is actively involved in various development projects, including education, healthcare, and social welfare. Through her schools, hospitals, and charitable organisations, the Church provides vital services to communities across the country, helping to improve the lives of millions of Nigerians.

Embracing the Future with Hope

As the Nigerian Church looks to the future, she must continue to embrace the trends and predictions that will shape her role in society. It is most expedient to adopt positive trends and foster its ethical engagements and usage without relegating the place of God and human dignity. The Church should continue to be a force for good in Nigeria, inspiring hope and bringing positive change to the lives of millions. The future of the Catholic faith in Nigeria is bright and full of opportunities to have a positive impact on society. By taking on her place in promoting national unity, peace, and development, the Church can continue to be a beacon of hope and a source of inspiration for all Nigerians.

Preparing Future Priests for Ministry

As the Church in Nigeria looks to the future, it's essential to consider how to prepare future Priests for ministry. This requires a deep understanding of the challenges and opportunities that lie ahead, as well as the commitment required in forming Priests who are equipped to meet the needs of the Nigerian Church in contemporary times.

Future Priests are the backbone of the Church, tasked with leading and shepherding the faithful. To prepare them for this crucial role, it is essential that they are formed in a deep understanding of their faith and the teachings of the Church. This includes a strong foundation in Scripture, Tradition, and the Magisterium of the Church, as well as a familiarity with the documents of the Second Vatican Council.

Scripture is the Word of God, and future Priests must be well-versed in her teachings and be able to apply them to the challenges of the modern world. They must also be firmly grounded in the Church's tradition of interpreting and transmitting the Gospel message over the centuries. They must also be faithful to the Magisterium, the educational authority of the Church, as set out in the document *Dei Verbum* (1965).

The documents of the Second Vatican Council are fundamental to understanding the mission and identity of the Church in the modern world. Two key documents, *Lumen Gentium and Nostra Aetate,* provide a framework for understanding the Church's role in the world and her relationship with other religions. The Church's dogmatic constitution, *Lumen gentium*, emphasises that the Church is the people of God and emphasises the role of all believers in the Church's mission. *Nostra Aetate*, the statement of the Church's relations with non-Christian religions, calls for dialogue and cooperation with people of other faiths and promotes understanding and mutual respect.

It is not enough for future Priests to simply understand their faith theoretically. They must also be able to apply this understanding to the challenges of the modern world. This includes issues of social justice, the environment, and bioethics. Future Priests must be able to address these issues thoughtfully and compassionately, drawing on the rich traditions of Catholic social doctrine and moral theology. They ought to be equipped and armed with modern trends and knowledge to make them effective pastorally and engaging with the time to lead the people of God.

Interaction with Cultural and Social Realities

Prospective Priests must be prepared to engage with the cultural and social realities of Nigeria. This entails a deep appreciation and understanding of the diverse traditions and customs of the Nigerian people. They must take into account the nuances of Nigeria's diverse cultures and recognise that these traditions are deeply embedded in the fabric of society.

Sensitivity to Cultural Diversity

Nigeria is a country with great cultural diversity. More than 250 ethnic groups live in the country, each with its own customs and traditions. Prospective Priests must be able to embrace these differences and serve people from all walks of life effectively. This requires an openness to learning and respecting the traditions of others, even those that may be different from your own.

Awareness of Social and Political Issues

In addition to cultural diversity, future Priests must also be aware of the social and political issues facing Nigeria. These include issues such as poverty, corruption, and ethnic and religious tensions. Understanding these issues will equip future Priests to better meet the needs of their communities and work for positive change.

Effective Communication and Pastoral Care

Effective communication is essential. They must be able to communicate effectively with people from all backgrounds, using language and concepts that are familiar and relatable. This requires a willingness to listen and learn from others, as well as the ability to adapt their message to different audiences.

Relevance and Meaningfulness of Pastoral Care

Ultimately, the goal of engaging with cultural and social realities is to provide pastoral care that is relevant and meaningful to the people of Nigeria. This means being able to address the spiritual, emotional, and practical needs of individuals and communities in a way that is sensitive to their cultural context. By doing so, future Priests can help to build a Church that is truly inclusive and welcoming to all.

Formed in a Spirit of Missionary Discipleship

Preparing future Priests in Nigeria requires a deep formation in missionary discipleship, embodying the call to go out to the peripheries, preach the Gospel to all nations, and make disciples of all people. This formation is rooted in the teachings of Jesus, who commanded His disciples to *"go and make disciples of all nations"* (Matthew 28:18-20).

Missionary discipleship begins with a willingness to go out to the peripheries, to those on the margins of society. This requires a deep sense of empathy and compassion for those who are suffering or marginalised. Future Priests must be willing to step out of their comfort zones and engage with people who may be different from themselves.

Preach the Gospel

The core of a Priest's mission is to proclaim the Gospel message. This includes not only preaching from the pulpit but also living the Gospel in our daily lives. Future Priests must be faithful witnesses of the faith, showing through their words and actions the love and mercy of Christ to others.

Recruiting Students

Another key aspect of missionary discipleship is the call to make disciples of all people. This includes not only leading people to the faith but also helping them grow in their relationship with God. Prospective Priests should be able to accompany others on their faith journey, providing guidance and support along the way.

Risk and Innovation

Missional discipleship often requires risk-taking and innovation in ministry. Future Priests must be willing to try new approaches to evangelization, use new technologies, and reach new groups of people. This requires a willingness to break out of the existing comfort zone and be open to new opportunities and challenges.

Open to New Opportunities and Challenges

Future Priests must be open to new opportunities and challenges. They must be willing to adapt to changing situations and accept new ways of thinking and acting. This requires a humble spirit and a willingness to learn from others.

Sense of Communion and Collaboration

Future Priests must be formed in a sense of communion and collaboration. This means being part of a united and supportive presbyterate and being willing to work together with other Priests, religious, and laypeople to build up the Church in Nigeria (Presbyterorum Ordinis, 1967). They must be able to listen to and learn from others and work collaboratively to achieve common goals.

In conclusion, preparing future Priests for ministry in Nigeria requires a deep understanding of the Church's teachings, sensitivity to the country's cultural and social realities, a spirit of missionary discipleship, and a sense of communion and collaboration. By forming Priests in these ways, the Church in Nigeria can continue to thrive and grow and be a beacon of hope and joy for all people.

The Role of Lay People in the Growth of the Church's Mission

The Second Vatican Council profoundly reshaped the understanding of lay participation in the Church. The Council's decree, Apostolicam Actuositatem (Decree on the Apostolate of the Laity), emphasises that laypeople share in the Church's mission by virtue of their Baptism and Confirmation. It states,

"The laity derive the right and duty to the apostolate from their union with Christ the head" (Vatican II, 1965. 3). Lumen Gentium (Dogmatic Constitution on the Church) further clarifies that laypeople are called to make the Church present and operative in places where only they can reach. "The laity have their own special vocation to make the Church present and fruitful in those places and circumstances where it is only through them that she can become the salt of the earth" (Vatican II, 1964. 33).

The role of lay people in the Catholic Church has evolved significantly, particularly in the context of the Church's mission. The role of laypeople in the Church's mission is both essential and expansive. Grounded in theological principles and enriched by historical developments, lay participation manifests in various practical ways that significantly contribute to the life and mission of the Church. As the Church continues to grow, the active involvement of laypeople will remain crucial in fulfilling her evangelical and social mission.

Reflecting on the role of laypeople in the Church's mission, I am inspired by the diverse ways in which the laity contributes to the vitality of the Church. Their involvement not only enriches the Church but also ensures that the faith remains vibrant and relevant in all areas of life. I recognise the profound responsibility and opportunity they have to live out the faith authentically and to be agents of transformation in the world. Lay people play a pivotal role in the Church's mission, contributing their diverse gifts, talents, and experiences to enhance the spiritual and communal life of the Church in Nigeria.

Active Participation in the Church

The laity are not merely onlookers but are actively called to engage in the Church's life. Their participation transcends attending services or Mass; they are integral to the liturgical, catechetical, and evangelical facets of the Church. The Second Vatican Council vividly calls laypeople to utilise their gifts in the service of the Church, contributing uniquely to her mission both within ecclesial settings and in the broader world (Apostolicam Actuositatem, 1966).

This active involvement includes volunteering in parish ministries such as teaching catechism, participating in choir, and assisting in liturgical preparations and celebrations. Lay individuals also take on leadership roles in parish councils and committees, influencing decision-making processes and the implementation of church programs.

Witnessing to the Gospel in the World

Lay people embody the Church's presence in the wider community. They are called to witness to the Gospel through their lives, actions, and words. This mission is vividly described in Matthew 5:13-16, where Jesus calls His followers to be the 'salt of the earth' and the 'light of the world'. Through their everyday living, lay faithful are to influence society positively by upholding values such as integrity, fairness, and compassion and embodying Christ's teachings in their interactions and endeavours anywhere they find themselves.

Promoting Social Justice and Human Rights

The Church recognises the laity's powerful role in advocating for justice and human rights. Guided by the principles of Catholic social teaching, lay people are urged to stand with the vulnerable and marginalised. This advocacy involves addressing systemic injustices and working towards transformative change, aligning with the prophetic call to justice found in Micah 6:8.

In Nigeria, where issues such as poverty, inequality, and discrimination persist, the laity's engagement in social justice can manifest in supporting charitable organisations, participating in community upliftment projects, and advocating for policies that protect human dignity and promote equity.

Collaboration with the Clergy and Religious

Effective mission work requires collaboration between the laity and the ordained clergy. This partnership leverages the distinct vocations and charisms of each group, fostering a richer and a more comprehensive approach to ministry. In pastoral care, lay professionals bring skills in counselling, administration, and education that complement the theological and sacramental roles of Priests and religious.

This collaborative spirit is essential for a holistic ministry. It ensures that the Church responds adequately to the diverse needs of her flock and extends her reach into the community. Various Church documents encourage such partnerships, emphasising mutual respect and shared responsibility in the Church's mission.

The biblical foundation for lay involvement is robust, anchored in the New Testament's portrayal of the Church as the Body of Christ, where each member plays a crucial role (1 Corinthians 12:12-27). In 1 Peter 2:9, lay Christians are described as a 'chosen race, a royal priesthood, a holy nation, God's own people,' called to proclaim the Excellences of Him who called them out of darkness into His marvellous light. This passage highlights the universal call to holiness and mission bestowed on all the baptized.

The role of lay people in the Church's mission is indispensable for the growth and effectiveness of the Church in Nigeria. Their active participation in the liturgical, pastoral, and evangelical aspects of Church life, combined with their witness to the Gospel in daily life and commitment to social justice, equips the Church to be a vibrant witness of God's kingdom. As lay people fulfil their call to holiness and service, they ensure that the Church remains a relevant, dynamic force for good in the world, truly reflecting the face of Christ to all they encounter.

Secularization and its Implications for the Christian Faith

Secularization, the process by which religious beliefs, practices, and institutions lose their significance in society, poses significant challenges for the Christian faith in Nigeria. This phenomenon is not unique to Nigeria but it is part of a global trend where the influence of religion in public life is diminishing.

Understanding Secularization

Secularization is often associated with the rise of modernity and the influence of science, technology, and rationalism. It entails a shift away from religious explanations of the world towards secular ones, emphasising human reason and empirical evidence. In Nigeria, secularization manifests in various ways, including declining religious observance, the rise of secular ideologies, and the marginalisation of religious values in public discourse.

Implications for the Christian Faith

1. Erosion of Religious Identity: Secularization can lead to a weakening of religious identity among Christians, especially the younger generation, who are exposed to secular ideas through education, media, and global influences.

2. Decline in Religious Practice: As society becomes more secular, there will be a decline in religious practice, such as attendance at religious services, participation in religious rituals, and adherence to religious teachings.

3. Challenges to Moral Values: Secularization can challenge traditional Christian moral values, particularly in areas such as sexuality, marriage, and the sanctity of life, leading to conflicts between religious teachings and secular ethics.

4. Loss of Influence: As religion loses its influence in public life, Christian institutions may find it challenging to engage with secular authorities and promote Christian values in society.

5. Opportunities for Dialogue: Despite its challenges, secularization also presents opportunities for dialogue between the Church and secular society. By engaging in dialogue, the Church can better understand secular perspectives and present her teachings in a way that resonates with secular audiences.

Responding to Secularization

1. Catechesis and Education: The Church can respond to secularization by providing strong catechesis and education that equips Christians to understand and articulate their faith in a secular context.

2. Engagement with Culture: Christians can engage with secular culture by promoting Christian values in the arts, media, and public discourse, offering a Christian perspective on contemporary issues.

3. Interreligious Dialogue: Engaging in dialogue with other religious traditions and secular ideologies can help Christians understand secular perspectives better and find common ground for cooperation.

4. Social Outreach: The Church can respond to secularization by engaging in social outreach and advocating for justice and peace, demonstrating the relevance of Christian values in addressing social issues.

In Romans 12:2, Apostle Paul exhorts Christians not to conform to the pattern of this world but to be transformed by the renewing of their minds. This passage reminds Christians of the importance of maintaining their faith in the face of secular influences and encourages them to seek renewal through a deeper relationship with God.

Strategies For Sustaining Faith in Changing Times

Sustaining the Catholic faith in Nigeria's ever-changing socio-cultural landscape presents both challenges and opportunities. The Catholic Church, with her rich tradition and profound teachings, has the potential to address these challenges by adopting innovative strategies while remaining rooted in its core values.

1. Emphasise on Personal Spirituality and Relationship with God

A fundamental strategy for sustaining faith is to encourage personal spirituality and a deep, personal relationship with God. In the Gospel of John, Jesus emphasises the importance of abiding in Him. *"I am the vine; you are the branches. If you remain in me and I in you, you will bear much fruit; apart from Me, you can do nothing"* (John 15:5). This relationship is nurtured through prayer, meditation, and regular participation in the sacraments. Priests can lead by example, demonstrating the power of a personal relationship with God through their own spiritual practices. Encouraging parishioners to cultivate their personal spirituality can help them find strength and guidance in their faith, especially during challenging times.

2. Leverage on Technology for Evangelization and Community Building

In this digital age, technology offers unprecedented opportunities for evangelization and community building. The Church can harness social media, online platforms, and digital tools to reach a broader audience and engage with parishioners in meaningful ways. The Vatican's document *Inter Mirifica* highlights the importance of media in modern evangelization. "The Church recognises that these media, if properly utilised, can be of great service to mankind" (Inter Mirifica, 2). Creating engaging and relevant online content, such as live-streamed masses, faith-based webinars, and social media posts, can help maintain a connection with parishioners. Digital platforms can facilitate virtual community gatherings, fostering a sense of belonging even when physical gatherings are not possible.

3. Foster a Culture of Lifelong Learning and Catechesis

Continuous faith education is essential for sustaining faith. The Catechism of the Catholic Church emphasises the importance of catechesis in the life of the Church. "The Church's mission is to foster, awaken, and sustain faith" (Catechism of the Catholic Church, 6). Priests and lay leaders can organise regular catechetical programs that cater to different age groups and levels of understanding. Adult faith formation programs, Bible study groups, and discussion forums can provide opportunities for parishioners to deepen their understanding of Catholic teachings. By fostering a culture of lifelong learning, the Church can equip her members to navigate contemporary challenges with a well-grounded faith.

4. Encourage Active Lay Participation and Leadership

The Second Vatican Council's document, *Lumen Gentium*, emphasises the role of the laity in the Church's mission. "The laity are made to share in the priestly, prophetic, and kingly office of Christ" (Lumen Gentium, 31). Encouraging active lay participation and leadership in parish activities can invigorate the Church community.

Laypeople can take on various roles, from leading prayer groups and organising community service projects to participating in parish councils and evangelization efforts. Empowering the laity to take ownership of their faith journey fosters a collaborative and dynamic Church environment.

5. Promote Social Justice and Community Service

Engaging in social justice and community service is a powerful way to live out the Gospel message and sustain faith. In the Gospel of Matthew, Jesus calls His followers to serve others. *"Truly I tell you, whatever you did for one of the least of these brothers and sisters of mine, you did for me"* (Matthew 25:40). The Church's commitment to social justice reflects her mission to uphold human dignity and promote the common good. Parishes can organise outreach programs, support charitable initiatives, and advocate for social justice causes. By addressing the needs of the marginalised and vulnerable, the Church can demonstrate the practical application of her teachings and inspire parishioners to live out their faith through action.

6. Strengthen Family Faith Formation

The family is often referred to as the "domestic Church," and it plays a crucial role in nurturing faith. The document *Familiaris Consortio* highlights the family's role in faith formation, "The

Christian family constitutes a specific revelation and realisation of ecclesial communion" (Familiaris Consortio, 21). Strengthening family faith formation can help ensure that faith is passed down through generations. Priests can support families by providing resources for family prayer, organising family retreats, and offering guidance on how to integrate faith into daily family life. Encouraging parents to take an active role in their children's religious education can create a strong foundation for lifelong faith.

7. Embrace Ecumenical and Interfaith Dialogue

In a diverse country like Nigeria, ecumenical and interfaith dialogue is essential for promoting peace and mutual understanding. The document *Nostra Aetate* encourages dialogue and collaboration among different faith communities. "The Church exhorts her sons, that through dialogue and collaboration with the followers of other religions, carried out with prudence and love... they recognise, preserve, and promote the good things, spiritual and moral, as well as the socio-cultural values found among these men" (Nostra Aetate, 2). By engaging in dialogue and cooperative efforts with other Christian denominations and religious groups, the Catholic Church can build bridges of understanding and work together towards common goals. This collaboration can also help address societal issues and promote a culture of peace.

8. Adapt Liturgical Practices to Contemporary Needs

While maintaining the integrity of Catholic liturgy, there is room for adaptation to meet contemporary needs. The document *Sacrosanctum Concilium* advocates for liturgical reform that fosters active participation: "The liturgy is the summit toward which the activity of the Church is directed" (Sacrosanctum Concilium,

10). Ensuring that liturgical practices are engaging and relevant can enhance the spiritual experience of parishioners. Introducing elements such as contemporary music, inclusive language, and interactive homilies can make the liturgy more accessible and meaningful to today's congregations. Additionally, celebrating liturgies that reflect the cultural diversity of the community can foster a sense of belonging and inclusivity.

9. Support Vocations and Clergy Well-being

Sustaining faith also involves supporting those who dedicate their lives to the Church. Promoting vocations to the priesthood and religious life is essential for the Church's future. The document *Pastores Dabo Vobis* emphasises the importance of fostering vocations: "The whole Christian community is responsible for the development of vocations" (Pastores Dabo Vobis, 41). Providing ongoing support and formation for clergy and religious can help them remain effective and committed in their ministries. Ensuring their well-being through spiritual, emotional, and physical care is crucial for their ability to serve their communities faithfully.

10. Address Contemporary Moral and Ethical Issues

The Church must engage with contemporary moral and ethical issues to remain relevant and provide guidance to her followers. Issues such as bioethics, social justice, environmental stewardship, and human rights require thoughtful and informed responses from the Church. The encyclical *Laudato Si'* by Pope Francis addresses the importance of environmental stewardship: "We need a conversation which includes everyone, since the environmental challenge we are undergoing, and its human roots, concern and affect us all" (Laudato Si', 14). By addressing such issues through preaching, teaching, and advocacy, the Church can help parishioners navigate these complex topics with a faith-based perspective.

11. Create Inclusive and Welcoming Church Communities

Creating an inclusive and welcoming church environment is essential for sustaining faith. The document *Gaudium et Spes* calls for the Church to be a community of love and acceptance: "The Church...is a sign and safeguard of the transcendent character of the human person." (Gaudium et Spes, 76). Priests and lay leaders can foster an environment where everyone feels welcome, regardless of their background or circumstances. This can be achieved through hospitality, active listening, and outreach programs that address the needs of all community members.

12. Strengthen Parish Community Life

Strong parish community life can provide a support network for individuals and families, fostering a sense of belonging and commitment to the Church. Organising social events, support groups, and community service projects can help build strong relationships among parishioners. Regular parish meetings and open forums can provide opportunities for parishioners to share their concerns, ideas, and feedback, ensuring that the community remains responsive to the needs of her members.

13. Promote a Culture of Gratitude and Stewardship

A culture of gratitude and stewardship can enhance the spiritual life of the community. Encouraging parishioners to recognise and appreciate the blessings in their lives fosters a positive and grateful attitude. Stewardship programs that promote responsible use of resources, including time, talent, and treasure, can help parishioners live out their faith in practical ways. This can include initiatives such as volunteer programs, financial stewardship education, and environmental sustainability efforts.

14. Build Resilience through Faith in Adversity

Building resilience through faith is crucial for sustaining belief in changing times. Apostle Paul reminds us of the strength that comes from faith. *"I can do all things through Christ who strengthens me"* (Philippians 4:13). Encouraging Christians to draw upon their faith during challenging times can help them develop the resilience needed to face adversity.

Priests can offer guidance on finding hope and strength in Scripture, prayer, and the sacraments. Sharing stories of saints and martyrs who persevered through trials can also inspire the faithful to remain steadfast in their faith. Additionally, creating support groups where individuals can share their struggles and receive encouragement can foster a sense of community and resilience.

Sustaining the Catholic faith in the changing socio-cultural landscape of Nigeria requires a multifaceted approach that integrates personal spirituality, technological innovation, lifelong learning, active lay participation, social justice, and more. By embracing these strategies, the Catholic Church can remain a vibrant and relevant force in the lives of her members, helping them navigate the complexities of modern life with a strong, enduring faith.

CONCLUSION

This Faith Must Not Perish

This book, "**Faith in Flux: Catholicism and the Dynamics of Witnessing in Today's Nigeria,**" has sought to illuminate the unique challenges and opportunities facing the Christian faith and the Church in this vibrant and complex nation. By examining the Nigerian context as a primary background, tracing the historical evolution of Christianity and Catholicism, and examining the multifaceted roles of the Catholic Church within society, one thing is clear: it is a narrative of resilience, transformation, and hope.

Nigeria, a land of diverse cultures and traditions, offers both fertile ground and formidable obstacles for the Catholic Church. The historical overview has shown us that, from the arrival of early missionaries to the establishment of robust local communities, Catholicism has woven itself into the social and spiritual fabric of the nation. The Church has not merely existed within Nigerian society but has actively been shaped by it, playing a crucial role in education, healthcare, and social justice.

Intertwining faith and culture remains a delicate dance as Catholics strive to harmonise traditional beliefs with the universal teachings of the Church. This cultural interplay has enriched the faith, bringing forth a unique expression of Catholicism that is distinctly Nigerian yet universally Catholic. While the Church treads carefully between spiritual leadership and temporal advocacy, the political involvement of Priests and the political participation of Catholics both highlight the Church's dedication to justice and peace.

The rise of digital ministries marks a new frontier for evangelization in this digital age. The Church must embrace these tools to reach a tech-savvy generation, ensuring that the message of Christ remains relevant and accessible. The dynamics of the Christian faith in Nigeria today, influenced by the rapid growth of Pentecostalism, call for an even more profound witness to the Catholic faith's depth and richness. This is a call for collaboration across Christian denominations to promote unity and a common purpose in a fragmented world.

The role of the lay faithful in the Church's mission cannot be overstated. Laypeople are not mere spectators but active participants in the life and mission of the Church. Their involvement in evangelization, social justice, and parish leadership is vital to the Church's vibrancy and growth. Looking ahead, the future of the Catholic faith in Nigeria will depend significantly on how well the laity and clergy can collaborate, innovate, and adapt to an ever-changing landscape.

As I reflect on the content of this book, I am filled with both concern and hope. The challenges are real and numerous: cultural tensions, political instability, the lure of secularism, and the rapid changes brought by digital technology. However, these challenges also present opportunities for renewal and revitalization. The Catholic Church in Nigeria stands at a crossroads, and both laypeople and clergy must rise to the occasion.

We must brace ourselves to preserve and transmit the deposit of faith with unwavering fidelity and creative engagement. This is a call to every Catholic in Nigeria to deepen their commitment to Christ, to live out the Gospel with courage and compassion, and to be witnesses to the transformative power of faith in every sphere of life. The future of Catholicism in Nigeria rests in our hands, and with God's grace, we can navigate this journey with hope and determination.

Looking forward, there is both hope and expectation. It is hoped that the efforts of the faithful of today will plant the seeds for a strong Catholic presence in Nigeria in the future and that each believer's dedication to faith will be demonstrated by deeds that speak of justice, love, and unwavering faith in God's providence. The path ahead will undoubtedly face obstacles, but the enduring spirit of the Catholic Church, guided by her Priests and laity, promises a future where faith not only endures but thrives, illuminating the path for generations to come.

Let us go forth with a renewed sense of mission, ready to face the future with the same spirit of faith and perseverance that has brought us this far. Together, we can ensure that the light of Christ continues to shine brightly in Nigeria, illuminating the path for generations to come. It is imperative that this rich tradition of the Catholic faith and leadership does not perish but is instead rejuvenated and strengthened. This call to action is directed not only to the clergy but to every member of the Christian community. Each is tasked with the mission to foster a faith that actively engages with the world to promote justice, peace, and reconciliation and, ultimately, the salvation preached by Christ Himself on every available media and platform. The community must rise to support educational initiatives, participate in civic life, and extend the teachings of Christ into every corner of societal interaction.

Every Catholic has a task: to carry forward the Church's legacy, be a pillar of community leadership, and guard spiritual and moral truths.

References

Adogame, A., *The Public Face of African New Religious Movements in Diaspora: Imagining the Religious' Other',* Ashgate Publishing, 2010.

Anderson, A. *African Reformation: African-Initiated Christianity in the 20th Century.* Africa World Press, 2001.

Ayegboyin, D., & Ishola, A., Christianity in Nigeria: A Historical Perspective. Ibadan: University Press, 2011.

Cahn, D. D., & Abigail, R. A. (2014). *Managing Conflict through Communication.* Pearson.

Catholic Bishops' Conference of Nigeria (CBCN). (2017). *Pastoral Letter on Religious Tolerance and Coexistence.* Abuja: CBCN.

Catholic Bishops' Conference of Nigeria. (2021). *Communiqué: National Issues and the Church's Response.* Retrieved from https://cbcn-ng.org/

Catholic Bishops' Conference of Nigeria. *Communiqué: National Issues and the Church's Response* (2021). Retrieved from https://cbcn-ng.org/

Catholic Bishops' Conference of Nigeria *Pastoral Letter on the State of the Nation,* 2017.

Catholic Laity Council of Nigeria (CLCN). (n.d.). About Us. Retrieved from https://www.catholiclaitynigeria.org/about-us

De Dreu, C. K. W., & Gelfand, M. J. (Eds.). The Psychology of Conflict and Conflict Management in Organisations. Lawrence Erlbaum Associates, 2008.

Doeme, O. D. *Address to the United States Congress,* 2015.

Economist Intelligence Unit. Nigeria Country Report, 2022.

Ehusani, G. *An Afro-Christian Vision: Ozovehe* University Press of America, 1991.

Falola, T. *Culture and Customs of Nigeria.* Greenwood Press, 2001.

Fisher, R., Ury, W., & Patton, B. *Getting to Yes: Negotiating Agreement Without Giving In*, Penguin Books, 2011.

Folger, J. P., Poole, M. S., & Stutman, R. K. *Working Through Conflict: Strategies for Relationships, Groups, and Organizations*, Routledge, 2017.

Francis, *Message for the Celebration of the 50th World Day of Peace*, 2017.

Gifford, P. *Ghana's New Christianity: Pentecostalism in a Globalizing African Economy*. Indiana University Press, 2004.

Hackett, R. I. J., & Grim, B. J. *The Global Religious Landscape.* Pew Research Center, 2011.

Hastings, A. *The Church in Africa: 1450-1950*, Clarendon Press, 1994.

Isichei, E. (1995). *A History of Christianity in Africa: From Antiquity to the Present.* Wm. B. Eerdmans Publishing.

John Paul II. *Address to the Bishops of Nigeria on their "Ad Limina"*, 1998.

Kaigama, I. *Address to the Nigerian Catholic Community,* 2018.

Knights of St. Mulumba. *Mission and Vision.* Retrieved from https://www.ksmnigeria.org/mission-and-vision

Lutz, J. *The Catholic Mission in Nigeria.* Rome: Propaganda Fide, 1889.

McCoy, J., "The Catholic Church in Nigeria: A Study of Internal Conflicts," in *Journal of Religion and Culture*, 2018.

National Population Commission, Nigeria. (2020). Nigeria Demographic and Health Survey 2019. Retrieved from https://dhsprogram.com/pubs/pdf/FR359/FR359.pdf

Ojo, M. A., *The Catholic Church in Nigeria: A Historical Survey.* Lagos: Paulines Publications, 2013.

Onaiyekan, J., *Address to the Nigerian Catholic Community*, 2015.

Onaiyekan, J. *The Catholic Church in Nigeria: Past, Present and Future.* Lagos: Catholic Secretariat of Nigeria, 2004.

Open Doors. World Watch List: Nigeria, 2022.

Peel, J. D. Y. *Religious Encounter and the Making of the Yoruba.* Indiana University Press, 2000. "Ad Gentes". Second Vatican Council, 1965.

Pew Research Centre. *Religion and Public Life: The Future of World Religions*, 2021. Retrieved from https://www.pewforum.org/

Pew Research Centre. *Religious Composition by Country: Nigeria*, 2020.

Pope Francis, Address to the Nigerian Bishops' Conference, 2015.

Pope John Paul II. *Centesimus Annus,* 1991.

Presbyterorum Ordinis, Second Vatican Council, 1965.

Rahim, M. A., *Managing Conflict in Organisations,* Transaction Publishers, 2011.

Ukah, A., "The Intersection of Christianity and Traditional Religion in Nigeria." In Journal of Religion and Culture, 2012.

United Nations, Department of Economic and Social Affairs, Population Division. World Population Prospects, 2019. Retrieved from https://population.un.org/wpp/.

Church Documents and Encyclicals

"Dignitatis Humanae" (Declaration on Religious Freedom) in Second Vatican Council, 1965.

"Gaudium et Spes", Pastoral Constitution on the Church in the Modern World in Second Vatican Council, 1965.

"Inter Mirifica" (Decree on the Media of Social Communications) in Vatican II, 1963.

"Lumen Gentium" in *Dogmatic Constitution on the Church.* Second Vatican Council, 1964.

"Nostra Aetate" Declaration on the Relation of the Church to Non-Christian Religions. Second Vatican Council, 1965.

"Sacrosanctum Concilium" in Second Vatican Council, 1963.

Benedict XVI, *Message for the 45th World Communications Day*, 2011.

Catechism of the Catholic Church. (1994). Libreria Editrice Vaticana.

Francis, *Message for the 48th World Communications Day*, 2014.

John Paul II. *Christifideles Laici,* 1988.

Paul VI. *Evangelii Nuntiandi.* Apostolic Exhortation on Evangelization in the Modern World, 1975.

Peel, J. D. Y. *Religious Encounter and the Making of the Yoruba.* Indiana University Press, 2000.

Pope Benedict XVI, *Caritas in Veritate* (Charity in Truth), 2009.

Pope Benedict XVI, *Spe Salvi* (Saved in Hope), 2007.

Pope Francis, *Laudato Si'* (On Care for Our Common Home), 2015.

Pope Francis. *Evangelii Gaudium*, 2013.

Pope John Paul II, *Centesimus Annus* (The Hundredth Year, 1991).

Pope John Paul II, Familiaris Consortio (The Role of the Christian Family in the Modern World), 1981.

Pope John Paul II, *Laborem Exercens* (On Human Work), 1981.

Pope John Paul II, *Redemptoris Missio* (On the Permanent Validity of the Church's Missionary Mandate), 1990.

Pope John Paul II, *Sollicitudo Rei Socialis* (The Social Concern of the Church), 1987.

Pope John XXIII, *Mater et Magistra* (Mother and Teacher), 1961.

Pope John XXIII, *Pacem in Terris* (Peace on Earth), 1963.

Pope Leo XIII, *Rerum Novarum* (Rights and Duties of Capital and Labour), 1891.

Pope Paul VI, *Populorum Progressio* (The Development of Peoples), 1967.

Pope Pius XI, *Quadragesimo Anno* (After Forty Years), 1931.

www.ingramcontent.com/pod-product-compliance
Lightning Source LLC
LaVergne TN
LVHW091313150826
845673LV00006B/1627

* 9 7 8 9 7 8 6 0 9 0 7 8 8 *